W9-DDU-112

Ancient History
SIMULATIONS

Grades 5-8

Written by Max W. Fischer

Teacher Created Resources, Inc.
6421 Industry Way
Westminster, CA 92683
www.teachercreated.com
©1997 Teacher Created Resources, Inc.
Reprinted, 2006
Made in U.S.A.
ISBN 13: 978-1-57690-102-1
ISBN 10: 1-57690-102-5

Teacher Created Resources

Illustrated by
Phil Hopkins

Edited by
Walter Kelly

Cover Art by
Sue Fullam

José Tapia

Table of Contents

Introduction

Anyone who has spent much time at all as a middle school educator has heard this specific group of students voice the perpetual lament "Why do we have to learn this?" *Ancient History Simulations* has been designed to induce relevance between the distant past and the student's present existence.

Although cultures and circumstances may change over the centuries, *Ancient History Simulations* is predicated upon the concept that basic human nature is a constant which binds us together. The activities place students in meaningful classroom learning situations that replicate circumstances of significant events and/or cultures of antiquity.

Through the use of problem-solving scenarios, classroom simulations, and simulated review games, the 25 activities within *Ancient History Simulations* have been designed to merge higher level thinking skills with an affective learning approach. The book is a most valuable instructional tool that promotes critical thinking among students.

Ancient History Simulations allows the students of today to actively reflect upon the struggles and ambitions of people from several millennia ago and compare those struggles and ambitions to the frustrations and aspirations of the world today. The long and inspiring history of humankind has brought us to the conditions we live in today. Those conditions may not be ideal, but when they are viewed against the backdrop of our forefathers' great endurance and evolution, we are compelled to understand and often admire the ingenuity, courage, and progress of the human race.

Simulations of the type that appear in this collection bring to life the problems that challenged the peoples of yesterday, that trouble the peoples of today, and perhaps will prefigure solutions for the peoples of tomorrow. In these simulations students are brought to engage themselves in the great adventure of life—an adventure spanning the centuries, crossing ethnicity and region, and binding us all to membership in the human race.

Success with Simulations

The activities in *Ancient History Simulations* have been selected in order to get students involved with history by actually simulating conditions of a particular historical era within the limited confines of the school environment.

Whether you intend to use a simulation for the purposes of introduction, review, or as part of the closure process, it is well to establish procedures throughout each unit that will maintain consistency and organization. Suggestions on how to best utilize and store the units in this book follow.

Simulation Format

Each simulation begins with a lesson plan designed to assist the teacher with the preparations and procedures necessary and closes with valuable background information which connects the simulation to the historical events being studied. The lesson plan for each simulation follows this format:

> - **Title of Simulation**
> - **Topic**
> - **Objective**
> - **Materials**
> - **Preparation**
> - **Procedure**
> - **For Discussion** (where applicable)
> - **Background**
> - **Follow-Up** (where applicable)

Storing Simulations

As you use each activity, you will want to save the components of the simulation by using a readily available and well-organized system which will serve the future as well as the present. Labeled file folders or large manila envelopes can be easily sorted and organized by simulation units and kept in a file box. Pages that will be duplicated or made into overhead transparencies can be easily stored in the file folders or envelopes. Game cards, labels, etc., should be placed in envelopes or resealable plastic bags before storing them in their respective folders. If possible, use index paper or heavy stock for reproduced items such as game pieces that will be used over and over again. Laminating will help preserve these items.

Outside materials such as candy or plastic spoons should be readily available and noted on the outside of the activity folder to serve as a reminder that these items need to be accessible for the simulation.

Once the simulations have been organized into a file box, you will be prepared for each unit on a moment's notice.

Let the simulations begin!

Cooperative Learning Teams

Cooperative learning is an important instructional strategy because it can be used as an integral part of many educational processes. It is made-to-order for thinking activities. The cooperative learning process acts as a powerful motivational tool.

Many of the activities in this unit involve the cooperative learning process in a team effort to find solutions or come to conclusions regarding the simulations. With this in mind, consider the following information as you initiate team activities.

> ## Four Basic Components of Cooperative Learning

1. **In cooperative learning all group members need to work together to accomplish the task.**
   No one is finished until the whole group is finished and/or has come to consensus. The task or activity needs to be designed so that members are not just each completing their own part but are working to complete one product together.

2. **Cooperative learning groups should be heterogeneous**. It is helpful to start by organizing groups so that there is a balance of abilities within and between groups. Some of the simulations in this book, however, require a specific type of grouping for cooperative teams in order to achieve the simulation objective. Under such circumstances, a balanced, heterogeneous, cooperative learning team arrangement will not be appropriate for the success of the simulation.

3. **Cooperative learning activities need to be designed not only so that each student contributes to the group but also so that individual group members can be assessed on their performance.** This can be accomplished by assigning each member a role that is essential to the completion of the task or activity. When input must be gathered from all members of the group, no one can go along for a free ride.

4. **Cooperative learning teams need to know the social as well as the academic objectives of a lesson.** Students need to know what they are expected to learn and how they are supposed to be working together to accomplish the learning. Students need to process or think and talk about how they worked on social skills as well as to evaluate how well their group worked on accomplishing the academic objective. Social skills are not something that students automatically know; these skills need to be taught.

Grapes and Nuts

Topic

The Transition of Hunter/Gatherer Groups into Agricultural Societies

Objective

Students will be able to explain why agricultural societies were able to specialize their labors. They will also identify why nonagrarian peoples often coveted the wealth of agrarian societies.

Materials

- about two pounds of unshelled peanuts
- about two pounds of seedless grapes
- about one dozen five-ounce paper cups (two cups per student team)
- plastic sandwich bags
- "farmer" and "hunter/gatherer" role cards (page 8)

Preparation

1. Make two copies of the farmer role cards and enough copies of the hunter/gatherer cards for all but two of your students. Laminating these cards for future use may be a worthwhile idea.

2. After obtaining the various supplies, place about 30 peanuts into each of two paper cups.

3. Place about 30 grapes into each of the two cups.

4. Take the remaining grapes, leaving them on the stem, and separate them into small sections. Place these sections into individual plastic bags.

5. Take the bagged grapes and remaining peanuts and hide them in an appropriate location. Your actual classroom may not be the best spot for this. If the classroom is in close proximity to the outside grounds of the school, it may be possible to scatter the grapes and nuts in a general area outdoors. Teachers will have to use their best judgment as to where to place these edibles.

6. Be sure to have an assignment readied for the next day.

Procedure

1. With students in learning teams of four, randomly pass out the role cards. (Be sure to sufficiently disperse the two farmer cards in the stack so no one team ends up with both of them.)

2. The two students who receive the farmer cards garner a cup of peanuts and a cup of grapes for their teams. From this point on, these two teams need only work on the next day's assignment while leisurely munching on grapes and peanuts.

   (**Note:** *Some students may be allergic to peanuts and should not eat them.*)

Grapes and Nuts *(cont.)*

Procedure *(cont.)*

3. The remaining teams of hunter/gatherers are to search the prearranged area for their own grapes and nuts. Each team is to collect 30 grapes and 30 peanuts before being allowed to return to their team location to enjoy the fruits of their labors and commence their assignment.

4. With about 10 minutes of class time remaining, call an end to the search efforts. Question students as to how much of their next day's assignments they got done. It should be very evident that the farmer groups had a significant advantage in this regard. Ask students to compare this situation to early civilizations:

   • What advantage did agrarian societies have over hunter/gatherers? (They had more time to devote to other work. They were able to specialize.)

   • What kind of specialized activities did these agricultural people do? (metal-working, pottery, weaving of fabric, architect and building, government, trading, merchants, etc.)

   • Which type of society was able to accrue more wealth? (agrarian)

   • What type of organization might have become necessary to protect a society's wealth and well-being? (an army or some form of military force)

Background

The domestication of plants goes back some ten thousand years in the eastern hemisphere and close to three thousand years in the western hemisphere. The purposeful production of plants and livestock allowed humans to channel their energies into other endeavors after the Paleolithic Era. Free time for specialized labor was the key ingredient in development of the earliest civilizations.

The fertile river valleys that harbored the earliest agriculture, such as the Tigris and Euphrates in the Middle East, were often beset with turmoil as nomadic cultures tried to take advantage of the richness of the land through force.

Thousands of years later along the Mississippi River in North America, maize cultivation fostered native tensions as permanent sources of food pitted agrarian and hunter/gatherer people against each other.

"Grapes and Nuts" may not be suitable for every classroom. The instructor needs to meet ample spatial requirements in order to hide the food. The more area that is available for the activity, the more challenging it will be for the hunter/gatherer teams. The demands of this space may negate the value of the activity for individual teachers. Furthermore, depending upon which groups are selected to represent the sedentary farmers, the teacher may not feel comfortable leaving those students in order to supervise the others on the hunt for food. Another arrangement may be required whereby an aide or other responsible adult watches over the classroom while the teacher monitors the gathering of food.

Grapes and Nuts Role Cards

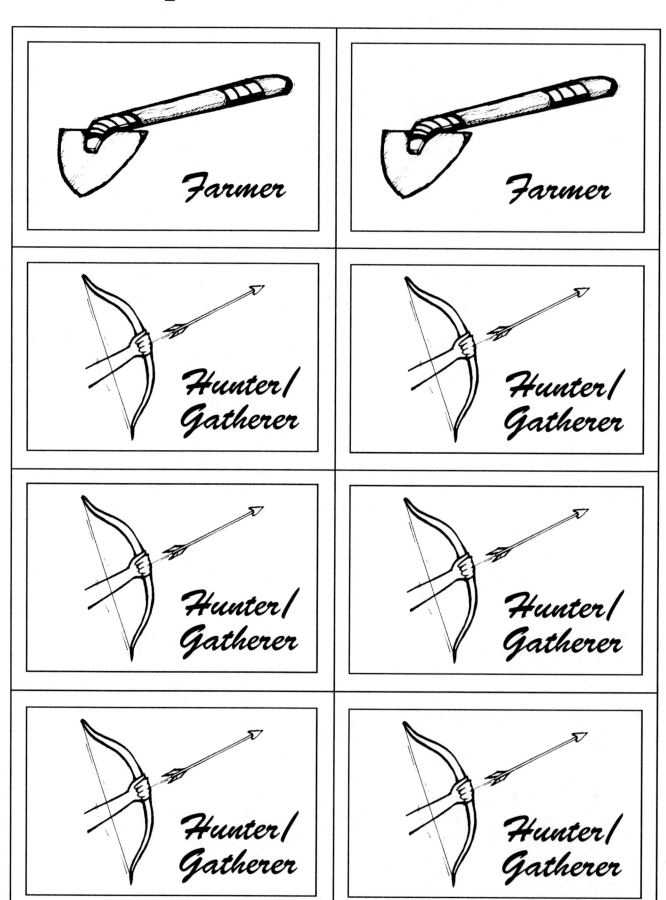

Squeezed Between the Rivers

Topic

Ancient Mesopotamia

Objective

Students will explain why Ancient Mesopotamia was so prone to invasion. They will relate how similar geographical characteristics affected the Persian Gulf War of 1991.

Materials

- a set of review questions about a recent lesson

Overhead Projection Version

- an overhead projector and marker
- an overhead transparency of the accompanying game board, "Squeezed Between the Rivers" (page 12)
- a die
- a small bag of candy for each star on the game board

Tabletop Version

- six to eight cardboard toilet tissue tubes
- a flat "paper football," the triangular type students have been making for ages
- a large, flat surface such as a table
- numerous square-cut pieces of paper or plastic squares to serve as tokens (the number to equal the number of review questions)
- several small, snack-size bags of candy (one for each cardboard roll)
- maps of Ancient Mesopotamia and the modern Middle East
- a map of the Balkans/Southeastern Europe

Preparation

1. Prepare your review questions over a previous lesson and obtain the candy.

2. Overhead Transparency Version: Obtain the overhead and make the transparency of the accompanying game board.

2. Tabletop Version: Obtain the cardboard tissue tubes and create the "paper football" by taking a 1.5" wide strip of paper about 6" long (3.75 cm x 15 cm) and folding it diagonally in alternating directions to end up with a triangular piece of paper. (See diagram.)

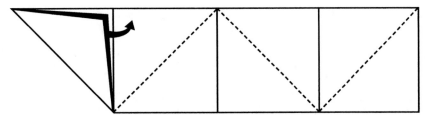

3. On the table place some books or notebooks about the outer perimeter of the table, similar to the diagram on page 13.

4. Place some paper X's about the table as indicated on the diagram.

Squeezed Between the Rivers *(cont.)*

Procedure

Overhead Version

1. Have the class divided into cooperative teams of about four students each.

2. Using the game board on the overhead, student teams may choose to start at any one of points A, B, or C.

3. On a rotational basis, teams attempt to answer review questions from a previous lesson. If they answer correctly, a die is rolled to see how many spaces they move on the gameboard from their selected starting point.

4. The object of the game is to capture those spaces marked with a star, which connotes riches. If a team lands on such a space, it is temporarily initialed by the teacher (with a marker) with the team's number or initials of its name.

5. If during a subsequent turn, another team lands on that very space, the new team replaces the previous team as owner of that space. (On subsequent turns, a team may move from its starred spot and still retain ownership of it as long as no other team lands on it during the interim between turns.)

6. Students may move in either direction, no matter what direction they may have undertaken initially.

7. When all review questions have been used, the activity is over. Any team in possession of a starred space receives a small bag of candy.

Tabletop Version

1. Have cooperative teams of four students each take turns answering review questions. With each correct response, give the team a paper or plastic token. Each of these tokens should be marked with the team's number or initials.

2. After the review questions have been covered, have teams return all tokens to a central place (a box or hat). Mix the tokens well.

3. At random, draw one token. The team whose token has been drawn will send one of its members to the table. There he or she will select any designated area with an X. From this spot the student will place the tip of the paper football onto the surface of the table, holding the top point with a finger of one hand. With the flick of a finger from the opposite hand, the student will try to propel the football into the cardboard tubes. Each tube that is knocked over represents one small bag of candy for the team.

4. Continue to randomly draw tokens one at a time until no more cardboard rolls are left standing.

For Discussion

1. No matter which version of the activity is used, ask students why they chose certain routes (overhead version) or positions (tabletop version) when they initiated their specific choices of action. The responses should revolve around the ease of the route or position in obtaining the candy.

Squeezed Between the Rivers *(cont.)*

For Discussion *(cont.)*

2. Refer to the map of Ancient Mesopotamia. Ask students what geographic features made it prone to attack from invaders. (It was relatively flat land with rich soil for food with no obstructing natural barriers.)

3. Using the modern map of the Middle East, ask a similar question. Why would it have been relatively easy for the American military to locate Iraqi targets during the Persian Gulf War of 1991? (Once again, flat terrain of the region along with sporadic desert vegetation gave a very open look to any major military actions that were undertaken. With the help of high tech imagery, the United States was often able to detect Iraqi military moves.)

4. If the teacher chooses, a comparison may be made to the American police efforts in Bosnia. Have students view a physical map of the Balkans region of southeastern Europe. How would the terrain indicated on this map be different from that of Iraq (Mesopotamia)? (It is mountainous with many places to hide military weapons. It would be easier to defend, or for Americans, harder to police.)

Background

"The land between the rivers," Ancient Mesopotamia, was one of the cradles of civilization because of its fertile soil, courtesy of the annual flooding of the Tigris and Euphrates rivers. This prosperous breadbasket was a prime target of invaders from all around Mesopotamia. From the nomadic herders from the deserts of the southwest to the herdsmen of the mountains to the north and east, numerous groups saw the plenty of the region as easy prey since there were no natural barriers to stop their incursions.

The earliest known settlements were villages in the foothills of northern Mesopotamia, established around 7,000 B.C. We have found traces of villages in the far south that date back to 5,000 B.C. Archaeologists know that somewhere around 3500 B.C. new people arrived in the region, but these scholars cannot be certain where the new arrivals came from. These people, known as *Sumerians*, built the world's first cities and developed what we think is the first system of writing, called *cuneiform*. The rich farmland between the rivers allowed a settled type of existence, giving people a chance to develop agriculture, trade, and the need for keeping written records.

In less than a thousand years, Semites (speakers of a language related to Arabic and Hebrew) conquered the Sumerians and ruled Mesopotamia until 539 B.C. when the Persians absorbed them into their empire. Alexander the Great, in turn, broke the Persian rule in 331 B.C. Since that time, the area has variously been dominated by Parthians, Romans, Arabs, Mongols, and Turks. Today it has become part of the modern nation of Iraq.

Even in the present day, the relatively flat plain of southern and central Iraq (along with satellite technology), gave the United States decided advantages when Operation Desert Storm was undertaken. Unlike the thick jungles of Vietnam or the mountainous terrain of Bosnia, the very openness of Iraq helped orchestrate a lightning-swift war of only one month.

Squeezed Between the Rivers *(cont.)*

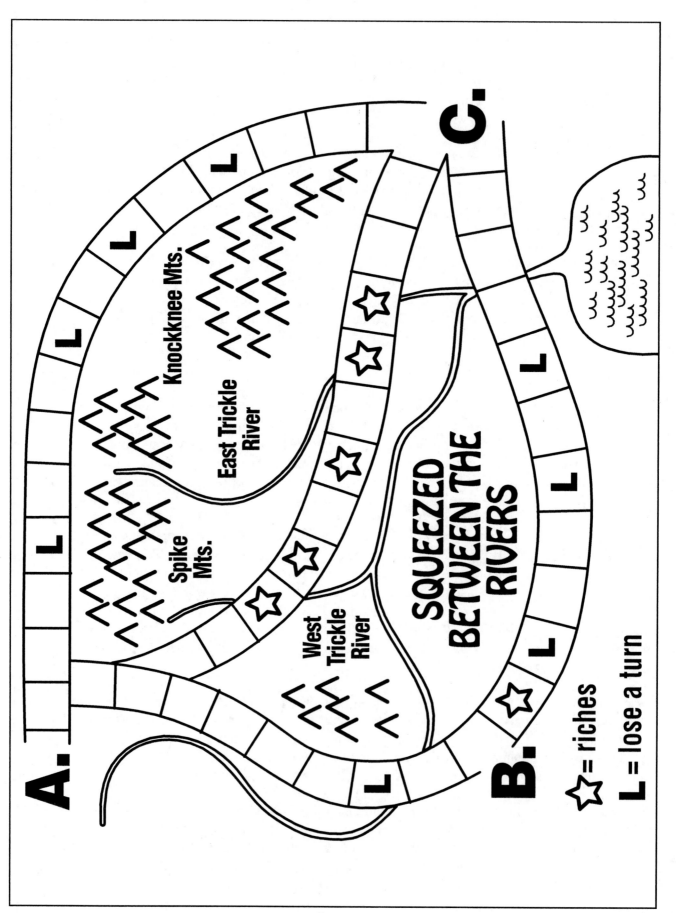

Squeezed Between the Rivers *(cont.)*

Tabletop Version

An Eye for an Eye

Topic

Hammurabi's Code

Objective

Students will compare Hammurabi's Code to Biblical Old Testament law and to our present Constitution. They will transfer constructs of his code to everyday life at school.

Materials

- copies of and/or excerpts from Exodus 21: 12–27, 23: 1–9 and Deuteronomy 19: 15–21 (preferably from the Living Bible or Good News Bible which have more modern English translations)

- easy student access to the school library or public library

Preparation

Make sufficient copies of the prescribed religious texts so as to provide one copy per student.

Procedure

1. Undertake a study of Hammurabi's Code. The instructor may have researched pertinent sources of information prior to the lesson's initiation, or he/she may have teams of students undertake this research. The resulting lesson should highlight not only the punitive aspects of this code of laws, but it should also give credit to its concern for humanity. (See Background, page 15)

2. After discussing the various elements of the Code of Hammurabi, have student teams put their collective heads together to develop similar laws for the everyday situations that arise at school. Emphasize to the class that in order to properly replicate a Hammurabi-type code, they should include as many protective laws as punitive laws.

   In other words, groups should not just concentrate on fiendishly clever punishments but should also concern themselves with rules that would protect weaker members of the school.

3. Have the student teams share their codes and promote class discussion as to whether the new rules would actually enhance the environment of the school.

4. Pass out the copies of the Old Testament text. Once again, student teams should work on locating passages that are similar to Hammurabi's Code. Exodus 21 will deal specifically with responsibilities and punishments while Deuteronomy 19 will touch on selected rights and the overall concept of justice. Have students compare/contrast the two ancient codes.

An Eye for an Eye *(cont.)*

Procedure *(cont.)*

5. Conclude with a discussion (team-oriented, whole class, or both) that attempts to compare our present law system to that of Hammurabi. Specifically, does our Constitution and Bill of Rights promote or reduplicate Hammurabi's Code? How are they similar? How are they different? Extra research time should be allotted for this section prior to actual class discussion.

Background

With some research, "An Eye for an Eye" does become an eyeful for students. They will realize that there is a bond across four thousand years and ten thousand miles that connects two distinctly different civilizations. Obviously, three to five class sessions would need to be devoted to the entire activity.

When Hammurabi took the throne of Babylon in 1792 B.C., there had already been various law codes in Sumeria (in the southern reaches of Mesopotamia).

While his was not the first codified set of laws, his review of the existing codes helped develop a truly enlightened legal system for the times. Although viewed as unduly harsh by our present-day standards, the punishments inflicted under Hammurabi's Code were considered amply just at the time. Not only did the punishment seem to fit the crime, the laws stretched across the entire social strata with higher classes yoked to an even higher standard of conduct. The following are a few of Hammurabi's laws with respect to punitive responsibilities:

- ❏ Should a builder build a house so poorly that it collapses on its owner, and the owner dies, the builder shall be put to death.

- ❏ A son who strikes his father shall lose his fingers.

- ❏ Should a person put out the eye of another, his eye shall be put out.

- ❏ If a patient dies after surgery, the surgeon shall lose his hand.

- ❏ If a freeman has broken another freeman's bone, they shall break his bone.

- ❏ If a freeman has destroyed the eye of a commoner or broken the bone of a commoner, he shall pay one mina (1–2 pounds of silver).

- ❏ If a freeman hired an ox and has destroyed its eye, he shall give one-half its value in silver to the owner of the ox.

Much of Hammurabi's Code dealt with basic rights for everyday people. It outlined rights and responsibilities for slaves, farmers, merchants, artisans, and nobility. In so doing, the structure of Mesopotamian society was anchored by a respect for the role of each part of society.

An Eye for an Eye *(cont.)*

Background *(cont.)*

Some interesting rights that were included in the code are as follows:

❏ If a soldier is taken prisoner during a war or is lost and unaccounted for and his wife marries another, when the soldier returns, he is to be able to reclaim his wife.

❏ If a man has lost interest in his first wife and marries another woman, he shall continue to financially support his first wife if she has not left his house and is still obedient to him.

Three to five hundred years later, Moses led the Hebrews out of Egypt and organized a similar law code. Exodus 21 and Deuteronomy 19 give sufficient flavor to its responsibilities and rights.

Certainly the penal codes at the federal and state levels of today do contrast remarkably to these ancient law codes.

Furthermore, the eighth amendment to the Constitution prohibits "cruel and unusual punishment." However, when one asks students to compare and contrast the ancient codes to those of our society, one must be sure to lead them along the lines of responsibilities, punishments, and rights. Most of the responsibilities remain intact today, and many of the rights would be honored as well. Punishments constitute the major area of contrast. However, in some areas of the Middle East, even today, similar punishments are still invoked.

Enrichment

Have student teams present oral presentations on certain aspects of Hammurabi's law or the Old Testament laws of the Hebrews. A team could focus on rights, responsibilities, and/or punishments. Poster-sized diagrams could be created. Other groups might interface with those teams to do a presentation on how contemporary law deals with the designated rights, responsibilities, or punishments in question.

I HAVE BROUGHT JUSTICE TO ALL MY SUBJECTS!

—HAMMURABI

Akbar's Dilemma

Topic

Religion of Ancient Mesopotamia

Objective

Students will identify the role religion played in the everyday lives of ordinary Mesopotamians. They will recognize that Mesopotamian religion stressed ritual for the here and now as opposed to any concern for the afterlife.

Materials

- the accompanying dilemma story, "An Act of God" (page 18)

Preparation

Make sufficient copies of the accompanying activity sheet so that each student has one.

Procedure

1. As an anticipatory set preceding a lesson on Ancient Mesopotamian culture or religion, have students read and discuss "An Act of God" in cooperative teams.

2. The student teams should focus on the questions that are included with the story. The entire class should discuss the situation to bring closure to the lesson.

Background

Ancient Mesopotamian religion revolved around a mythical theme of vengeful gods and goddesses. Man was viewed as a slave to their every whim and, as such, was responsible for keeping the gods happy. From exquisitely appointed temples and shrines to the continual sacrifices of beer, grains, and fruit, Mesopotamians viewed their role on earth as one of fulfilling the needs of the gods. The better they did this, the more successful their earthly pursuits would be.

To this end, numerous methods of fortunetelling arose. Interpretation of dreams, astrology, and the reading of animal organs were necessary measures in determining the will of the gods. The present was stressed, in part, due to the dismal view the Mesopotamians had of the afterlife.

The Mesopotamian view of immortality was a mere existence in some dingy underworld. It was nothing to work toward or look forward to. Therefore, no great expense was utilized in preparing the dead for burial. One's existence in the here and now was all that really mattered. To be successful, the gods had to be placated.

Akbar's Dilemma *(cont.)*

An Act of God

Akbar viewed the rubble that once had been his store. As the smoke from the charred ruins of this end of the city mingled listlessly with the steel-gray sky, he wondered where he had gone wrong. He had done everything according to plan. He had the priest advise him as to the exact type of chicken to kill. He had the most reliable fortuneteller read the bird's liver on the sacrificial pedestal at his local shrine for the gods.

Furthermore, he was assured that if he gave the gods 10 bushels of grain, 10 bushels of fruit, and several baskets of bread, his new store would have an excellent chance at making money. It was not an act of faith as much as it was the price of doing business. He could not afford to offend the gods. Before one mud brick of his store was put in place, he had painstakingly sought their blessings. It was how his father and his father's friends had begun all of their new business ventures. It was the way—priest, fortuneteller, gifts for the gods. Somehow, it had always seemed to work for them.

Yet a tremendous trembling of the ground had occurred during the night. Many people had been killed on this northern fringe of the city of Kish. Akbar's store was just inside the area of heaviest damage. Many buildings had collapsed, and numerous fires had started.

It finally dawned on Akbar that perhaps someone else was to blame. Perhaps another had offended the gods with a feeble sacrifice of stale bread and over-ripe fruit.

Unfortunately, Akbar and others had ended up paying for this foolish one's error in failing to render proper homage to the gods. He wondered aloud, "When will people learn that the gods must be paid off properly?"

Respond to the following questions:

1. Do you think Akbar was religious? If so, what did he worship?

2. In what kinds of "worship" activities was Akbar involved? Who was there to assist him?

3. Think of the kinds of worship activities that you may do as a part of your religion. How was Akbar's religion similar to or different from yours?

4. From what you read in this story, do you think Akbar's religion was concerned with any idea of an afterlife? Why or why not?

Trader's Circuit

Topic

Economics of Ancient Mesopotamia

Objectives

Students will identify major products and resources vital to Mesopotamian trade. They will compare Mesopotamian trade to our own capitalistic system.

Materials

- the accompanying set of trader's cards (pages 21 and 22)

Preparation

Create a deck of trader's cards for each team of four students. A deck consists of seven cards of each separate product or resource and one wild card for a total of 50 cards. Use heavy stock that can be laminated so the cards may be held for future use.

Procedure

1. After an initial lesson concerning Mesopotamian economics (see Background, page 20), have students divide into cooperative teams of four with each group having a deck of trader's cards. If there is an odd number of students, a group of five is preferable to a group of three.

2. The dealer within each team should shuffle the deck thoroughly and deal 12 cards per student on the team. Since there are two extra cards in the deck, the dealer and the person to his/her immediate left will receive an extra card each, so they will total 13 cards.

   No player may look at his/her hand until the dealer is ready to do likewise!

3. Once the dealer signals the go-ahead, cards may be traded by signaling for a particular number of cards only. Hand signals or oral commands may be honored, provided the player sends all of one kind of product/resource card in the transaction and that no mention of the product/resource is made.

4. The "Wild Card" comes into play in combination with six of a particular commodity to form a winning hand. (Seven of a particular kind also wins.)

5. The first player to complete such a product/resource "circuit" (actually a monopoly) calls out "Circuit complete!"

SIMULATION #5

Procedure *(cont.)*

6. For extended play, tally only the points of the winning hand which would equal the point value of a set commodity times how many cards of that product/resource were actually held. For example, a winning hand of seven "Jewelry" cards would be equal to 700 points. However, a hand of six "Jewelry" cards and the "Wild Card" is only worth 600 points. The "Wild Card" has no point value.

7. A basic strategy has the groups playing a practice hand followed by the initial scored round. If you wish, winners of the first round may meet head-to-head to determine the champion "trader" of the class in an abbreviated tournament.

For Discussion

Discuss with the class how this type of trading would be similar to our capitalist system of trade today.

Since capitalism refers to a system of open, competitive economics with the individualistic drive for profit, students should realize that Mesopotamian traders indeed were capitalists seeking any advantage they could attain.

Question students as to what advantage there is to gaining control of an entire resource in a general area. (Their monopoly would allow them to set the price of the resource without fear of competition.)

Background

"Trader's Circuit" is a very active simulation, and you may be hard pressed to maintain an appropriate noise level. Ideally, this activity works best at the end of the day, especially on a Friday or any day preceding vacation when students' natural penchant is to let off some steam.

While Mesopotamia was for the most part an agrarian society, artisans and merchants augmented its economy by meeting critical needs. Barley, sesame, and date palms were the main agricultural products. At the same time, pottery, textiles, jewelry, metal goods, and clay bricks were valuable manufactured goods.

Since the region was mostly void of stone and metals, trade was extremely important for the early Mesopotamians, for these items would be valuable to the building and manufacturing concerns. Through the Code of Hammurabi, it is known that there was a thriving capitalistic business class that incorporated many presumably modern methods of business—-credit lending, contracts, weights and measures, lending for interest, etc.

Trader's Circuit Trader Cards

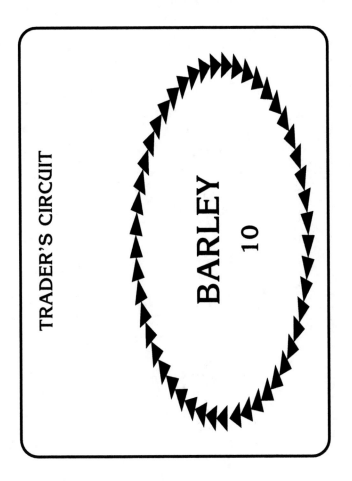

TRADER'S CIRCUIT

BARLEY
10

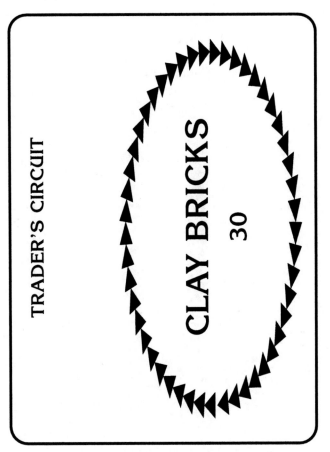

TRADER'S CIRCUIT

CLAY BRICKS
30

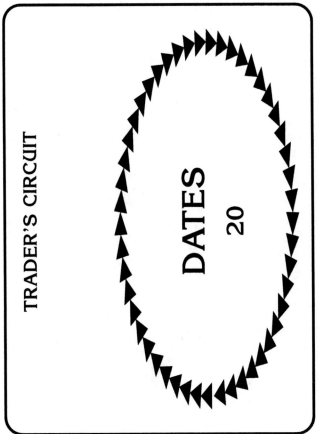

TRADER'S CIRCUIT

DATES
20

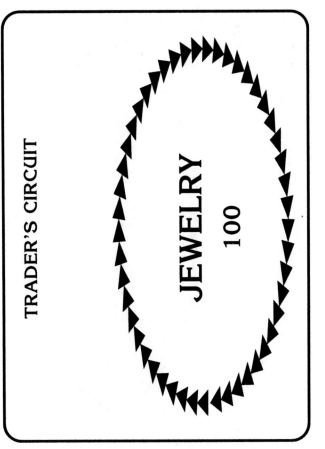

TRADER'S CIRCUIT

JEWELRY
100

Trader's Circuit Trader Cards *(cont.)*

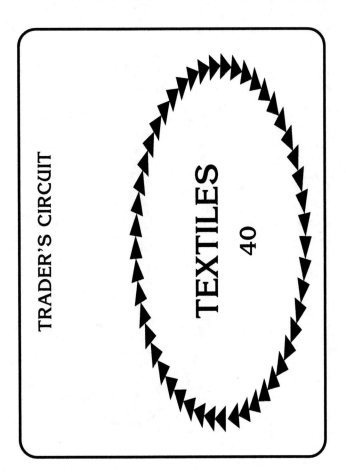

TRADER'S CIRCUIT

TEXTILES

40

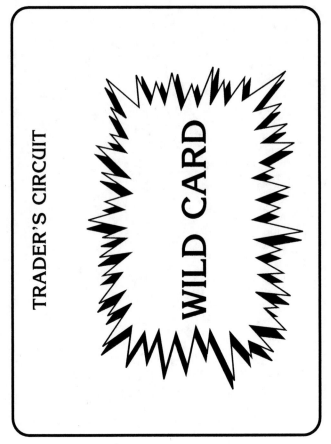

TRADER'S CIRCUIT

WILD CARD

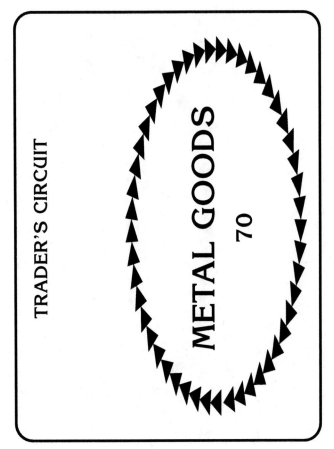

TRADER'S CIRCUIT

METAL GOODS

70

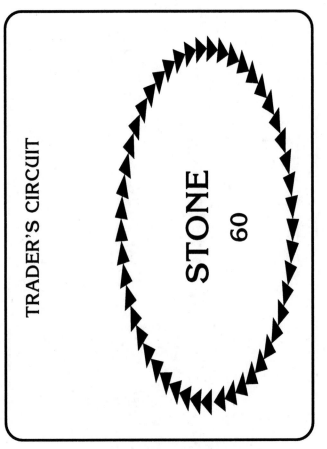

TRADER'S CIRCUIT

STONE

60

The Black Land

Topic

Geography of Ancient Egypt

Objective

Students will identify the geography of Egypt as the chief factor in Ancient Egypt's remaining relatively free from foreign influence and invasion.

Materials

- six to eight cardboard bathroom tissue tubes
- a flat "paper football," the triangular type students have been making for ages
- a large, flat surface such as a table
- a set of review questions about a previous lesson
- numerous square-cut pieces of paper or plastic squares to serve as tokens (the number equal to the number of review questions)
- several small, snack-size bags of candy (one for each tissue roll)
- maps of Ancient Egypt as well as modern Egypt

Preparation

1. Ready your review questions over a previous lesson and obtain the candy.

2. Obtain the tissue rolls and create the "paper football" by taking a 1.5" wide strip of paper about 6" long (3.75 cm x 15 cm) and folding it diagonally in alternating directions to end up with a triangular piece of paper, once the final fold is tucked in.

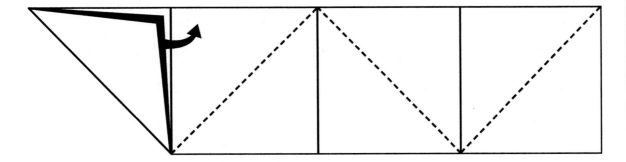

3. On the table, place a considerable number of books, notebooks, or other handy objects similar to the diagram on page 26.

4. Place a paper X on the table at the spot designated on the diagram.

The Black Land *(cont.)*

Procedure

1. Have cooperative teams of four students each take turns in answering the review questions. With each correct response, give the team a paper or plastic token. Mark each token with the team's number or name.

2. After the review questions have been covered, have teams return all tokens that were earned to a central collection spot (a box or hat). Mix the tokens well.

3. At random, draw one token. The team whose token is drawn will send one of its members to the table. There he/she will place the tip of the paper football on the X while holding the top point of the paper football with a finger of one hand. With the flick of a finger from the other hand, the person will try to propel the football at the tissue tubes. Each tube that is knocked over represents a bag of candy for that team.

4. Continue to randomly draw tokens one at a time until no more rolls are left, or when allotted time expires.

For Discussion

1. Unlike a similar activity in "Squeezed Between the Rivers," students should have a rather difficult time hitting their targeted tissue tubes in "The Black Land." Ask them what made this physical exercise so difficult. (There is but one spot from which to shoot the paper football.)

2. Refer to a map of Ancient Egypt (from either a textbook or classroom wall map). Ask "What made Ancient Egypt so easy to defend from invasion?" (Its geography gave it sufficient insulation—deserts to the west and east of the Nile River Valley, violent rapids several hundred miles south along the Nile, the Mediterranean Sea to the north. The only feasible military entrance was a narrow strip connecting the delta of the Nile with southwestern Asia.) "How might this geography have affected the culture of Ancient Egypt and the neighboring empires?" (It would have worked to keep Egypt isolated from other cultures and relatively stable to develop its own unique way of life.)

3. Referring to a map of present-day Egypt, the instructor may ask if the Egypt of today is similarly isolated. (Modern transportation and communications technology have overcome geographic barriers.)

24

The Black Land *(cont.)*

Background

The "Black Land" is what ancient Egyptians called the Nile Valley and the rich soil which sustained their lives. Conversely, the desert lands which sought to inundate them from the west and east were known as the "Red Land."

After the first pharaoh, Menes, united Upper and Lower Egypt, well-organized government and the geography of the land itself kept Egyptian civilization free of invasion and unwanted outside influence for almost fifteen hundred years.

This activity may be used as an anticipatory set to introduce ancient Egypt's cradled position along the Nile. It could also serve to reinforce the concept after one or several initial lesson(s) on the land of the Nile. If one chooses the latter, pay careful attention as to how quickly some students identify the analogous relationship between ancient Egypt's geographic characteristics and the daunting "paper football" challenge.

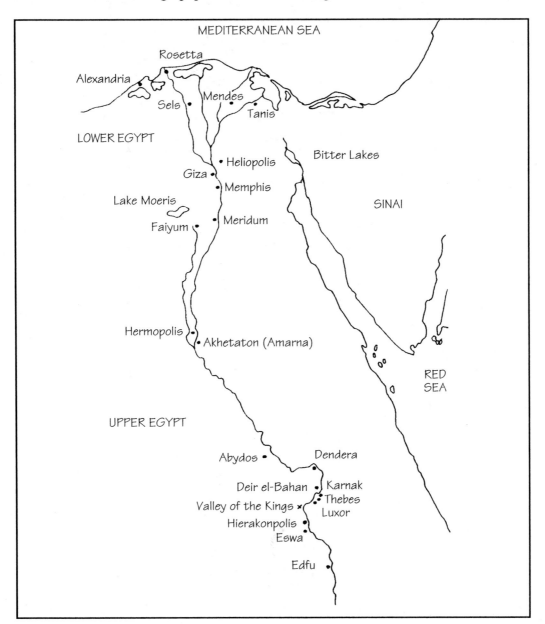

The Black Land *(cont.)*

Tabletop Version

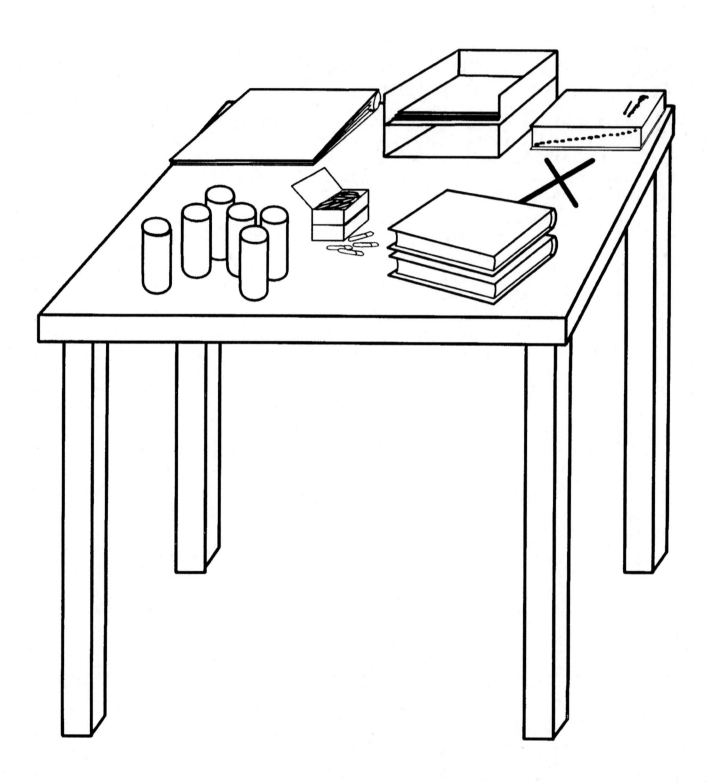

Re's Riches

Topic

Social Classes of Ancient Egypt

Objective

Students will identify the major socio-economic ranks within Ancient Egyptian society. They will also recognize the importance of each to the civilization.

Materials

- a large bag of M&M's or similar bag candy
- the accompanying role cards (pages 30 and 31)
- several plastic spoons (one for each student team)
- small paper cups (seven per team)
- larger (4–5 oz.) paper cups (a number equivalent to four more than the total number of student teams)
- four copies of Procedure, steps 2–4

Preparation

1. Procure the needed materials (cups, spoons, and candy).

2. Make sufficient copies of the role cards so that you will have one each of the following—PHARAOH, VIZIER, PRIEST, NOBLE—and enough PEASANT and CRAFTSMAN/MERCHANT cards to distribute among the rest of the class.

3. Produce four copies of Procedure, steps 2–4. It will serve as a script for students fulfilling specific roles.

4. Evenly distribute the candy into the large paper cups allotted for the student teams. (Be sure to have four empty large cups remaining.)

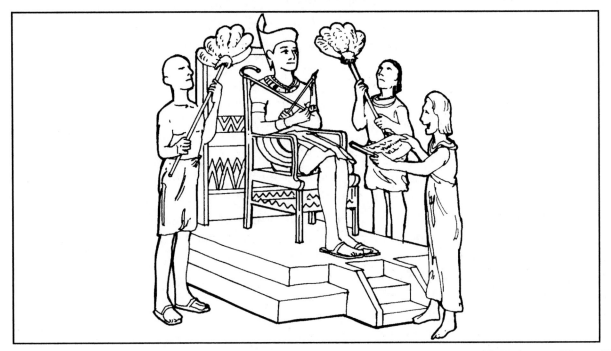

Re's Riches *(cont.)*

Procedure

1. Have students in cooperative learning teams of four. Shuffle the role cards and randomly pass them out. Those with the PHARAOH, VIZIER, NOBLE, and PRIEST cards should leave their respective teams and be seated near the front of the room. Each of them should be given a large paper cup of candy and a copy of steps 2–4 below.

2. From this point onward, the VIZIER takes over the simulation by ordering each of the following steps (A–E):

   A. One member of each group obtain seven small cups and a spoon for the group.

   B. Use your spoons to place all brown and tan candies from your cup into two separate small cups.

   C. Use your spoons to place all red, yellow, orange, green, and blue candies into separate small cups for each color.

   D. The great Pharaoh (name of student who drew the PHARAOH card), son of Re, almighty god of the sun, has need of your labors. Bring all brown and tan candies to Pharaoh and deposit them in his cup.

   E. Bring all yellow candies forward unto me, the Pharaoh's vizier, that I may ensure the will of the Pharaoh will be done throughout the government. (Students place the yellow candies into the VIZIER's cup.)

3. At this point, the PRIEST takes over and reads the following command:

   The great god Re needs to sustain his worship on earth and the worship of all gods under him. Bring all orange and green candies forward and place them in my cup.

4. Finally, the NOBLE issues the final command:

   As your immediate landlord, I expect to share of your labor. Bring all red candies forward and place them into my cup.

For Discussion

• All students may return to their seats and be free to enjoy the fruits of their labor, however large or small that may have been. Even though it may seem unfair to them at present, ask students if the peasants of Ancient Egypt would have felt it unjust to give their crops and labor away. (Pharaoh was a living god on earth, son of the omnipotent Re. Peasants, craftsmen, merchants, and the very land upon which they lived was owned by the pharaoh. It was their duty to obey the gods.)

• How was the lot of the craftsman and merchants different from that of artisans and merchants of Mesopotamia? (Mesopotamian craftsmen and merchants made up a rather rich and powerful segment of their society.)

• Since so much was done for and given to the pharaoh, what seems to have been the most important part of the average Ancient Egyptian's life? (Religion was very important. Fulfilling the Pharaoh's wishes was a meaningful way of entering into the afterlife. See "Connecting Osiris," page 32)

Re's Riches *(cont.)*

Background

The Nile River provided Ancient Egypt with enormous agricultural wealth. Sometimes several crops were harvested annually on the same rich alluvial soil. Since pharaoh was the god-king, all was owned by him.

Added to that, governmental officials required taxes of crops and labor in order to provide buildings for the pharaoh (usually tombs for his afterlife and those of his family and officials) and food for his court. Priests were in charge of the building and care-tending of the temples of the gods and naturally had to be supported. Finally, the aristocratic web that emanated from pharaoh and spread to whomever he shared his favor with throughout the land allowed nobility to exact crop taxes from peasants.

While artwork on ancient Egyptian artifacts depicts satisfied and healthy farm laborers, their reality was little more than bare subsistence. Any satisfaction would have been garnered from realizing that they were pleasing the gods and, therefore, would be entitled to some form of immortality.

Artisans and merchants of this era were also bound to either nobility or the priestly class. They produced and procured the necessary implements for the aristocrats and temples and were not able to rise much above subsistence.

Follow-Up

Working with the art teacher, you may wish to have students research appropriate headdresses of the Egyptian civilization and work to recreate those suitable to the roles presented in the activity. Students of various status may wear the headdresses during the activity.

Re's Riches Role Cards

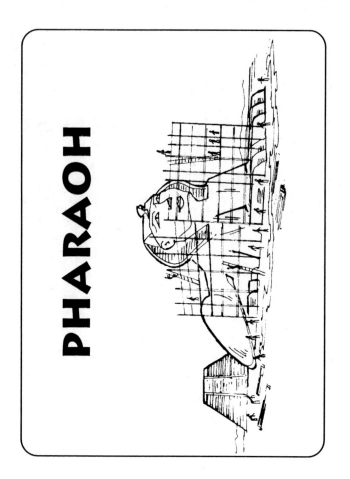

PHARAOH

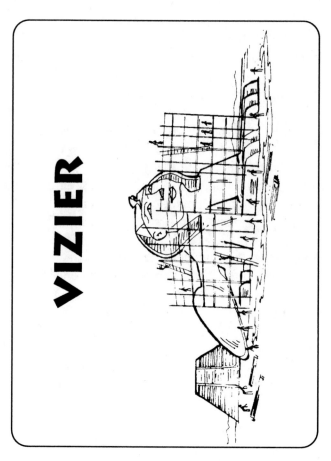

VIZIER

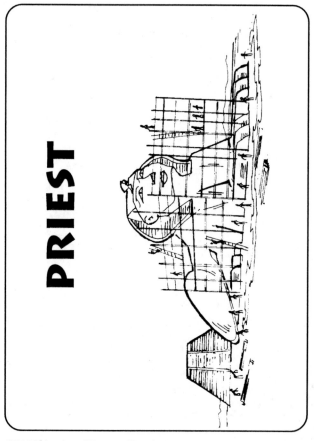

PRIEST

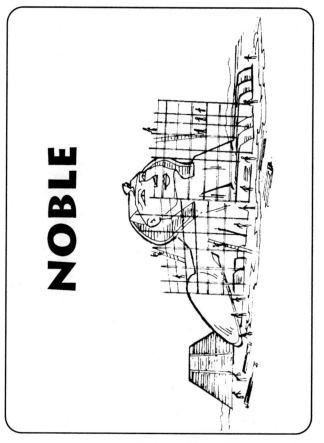

NOBLE

Re's Riches Role Cards *(cont.)*

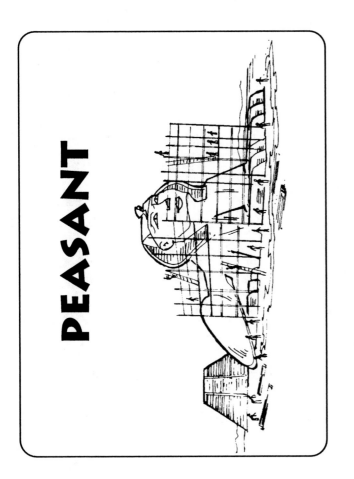

PEASANT

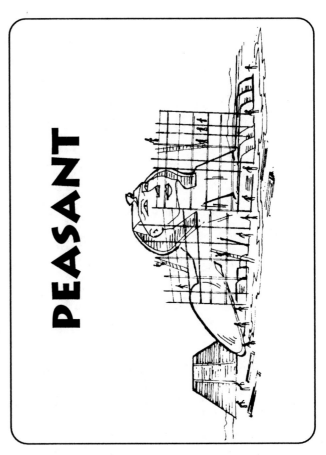

PEASANT

CRAFTSMAN/MERCHANT

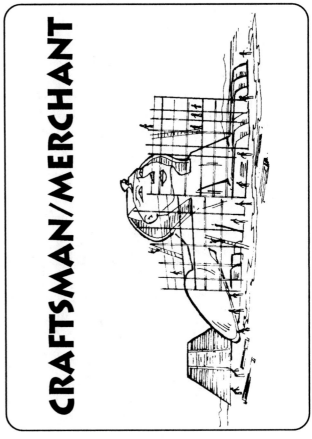

CRAFTSMAN/MERCHANT

Connecting Osiris

Topic

Religion of Ancient Egypt

Objective

Students will identify Ancient Egypt as the origin of the idea that moral worth was the key to eternal life.

Materials

- an overhead projector and transparency sheet
- the accompanying picture of Osiris (page 34)
- sealable (those with a zipper are preferable) plastic bags—one per student team

Preparation

1. Make an overhead transparency of Osiris.
2. Make copies of Osiris equal to the number of student teams within the class.
3. Cut each copy of Osiris into approximately 20–24 irregularly shaped pieces. (Each may be cut separately, or several copies may be cut together to expedite the process.)
4. Place pieces for each copy into separate plastic bags.

Procedure

1. Ask the students if they understand the concept of immortality or eternal life. Allow some discussion of their ideas of eternity.
2. Pass out the Osiris puzzle bags to each team.
3. Instruct students that they will unlock the "key" to the Ancient Egyptians' view of immortality as they work the puzzle in front of them. Project the image of Osiris on the overhead.

   Allow student teams time to complete their respective puzzles.

Connecting Osiris *(cont.)*

Procedure *(cont.)*

4. After groups have successfully completed their puzzles, share the importance of Osiris' legend with the students (See Background.) Have students compare the Egyptian version of eternity with that of the Ancient Mesopotamians. (See "Akbar's Dilemma," page 17.) Which one would be more favorable? (The Egyptians had a much more positive view of eternity than the Mesopotamians.)

Background

The idea that moral constitution, not material wealth, dictated eternal happiness started in Egypt about four thousand years ago. Its origin is in the legend of Osiris, one of the sons of Ra, who was killed and dismembered by his evil brother, Seth. Osiris's wife, Isis, gathered the various parts of Osiris' body, and he came back to life to serve as the god of the dead. He would determine the worthiness of any dead person by placing the person's heart on a balance offset with the weight of a feather. If the heart was light and good, it would balance, and the person would be welcomed into eternity. A heart malignant with wickedness would easily tip the scales, and that person would be thrown to a voracious monster to be devoured.

Follow-Up

Have students compile a list of values or virtues that they think are important. These lists may be developed and discussed in teams and/or whole class sessions.

The teacher may want to ask students to write a descriptive paper on what they perceive eternal life to be. They may cite religious beliefs or other references for their particular conceptions.

Connecting Osiris Picture

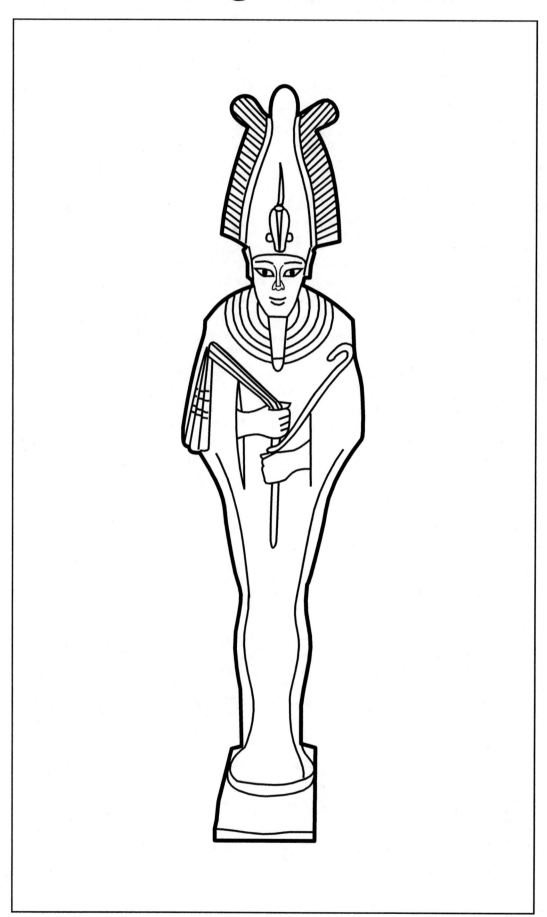

The World of the Phoenicians

Topic

Ancient Phoenicia

Objective

Students will recognize Ancient Phoenicia as a trading society that disseminated Egyptian and Mesopotamian culture throughout the Mediterranean region. They will solve map problems employing the use of scale.

Materials

- the accompanying map, The World of the Phoenicians (page 40)
- the accompanying set of action cards (pages 38 and 39)
- a pair of dice
- an overhead projector and transparency sheet
- a clear plastic lid (such as one from a yogurt container)
- a permanent marker
- a paper clip
- rulers (for students' use)

Preparation

1. Make one copy of The World of the Phoenicians Map for each student.

2. Make an overhead transparency of the map.

3. Make an overhead transparency for each page of the action cards. Cover the WILD CARD selections with small paper cutouts.

4. Make a directional spinner by using the permanent marker to create a compass rose on one side of the clear plastic lid. Bend out one end of the paper clip and carefully force it through the center of the lid/compass. Once through the lid, bend the clip back so it becomes parallel to the remainder of the clip on the other side of the lid. See the diagram on page 36.

   Give the clip a spin by flicking it with a finger to test its spinning ease. Some minor adjustments may have to be made in the clip's bend.

Procedure

1. With students grouped in cooperative teams, pass out a copy of the map to each student.

2. Randomly assign each team a numbered destination that appears on the map. The object of the game is to arrive at your team's destination before any other team arrives at theirs.

The World of the Phoenicians *(cont.)*

Procedure *(cont.)*

3. All teams will start from the Phoenician city of Tyre. On a rotational basis, each team will roll a pair of dice. The total number from the toss of the dice is the equivalent in hundreds to the miles of travel—a total roll of seven would equal 700 miles, a total roll of five would be 500 miles of travel, etc.

   Meanwhile, the instructor will have the directional compass/spinner projected overhead onto a screen. The teacher spins the compass to see in which direction that team will proceed. (Since it is obvious the Phoenicians routinely started in some westwardly direction, each team's initial turn shall be in some westerly direction of that team's choice. Subsequent turns will use the teacher-directed compass/spinner.)

4. Students use their rulers and the line scale on the map to deduce how far they travel on that particular turn in the designated direction.

5. If a team strays off its course too far because of an ill-fated spin of the compass, it can right its course by choosing an action card on its next turn.

   Once an action card has been chosen, it cannot be used by another team. No team may use more than two action cards. (**Note:** *Advise students that the blacked-out areas represent WILD CARDS which may have positive or negative effects on their trip.*)

6. The first team to reach their destination is declared the winner.

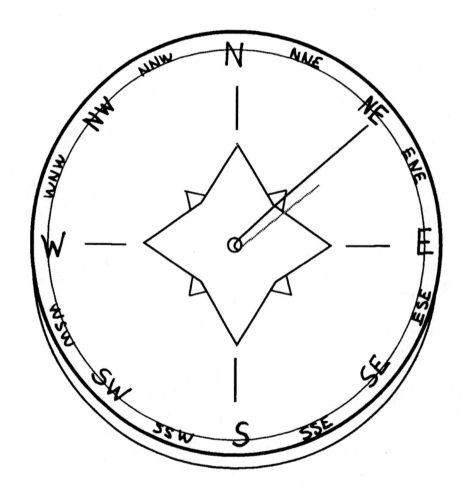

The World of the Phoenicians *(cont.)*

Background

Some three thousand years ago, Phoenicia was a small civilization made up of several city-states located where modern-day Lebanon exists today. Phoenicians were the most famous traders and mariners of Western antiquity. They set up colonies throughout the Mediterranean region from Cyprus to southern Spain.

The Phoenicians carried more than their notable exports of dye, glass, textiles, and metallic goods to other lands. They spread Egyptian and Mesopotamian culture throughout their travels, and they are forever linked with devising an alphabet. The Phoenician alphabet eventually served as a model for Greek and Roman letters.

Modern	A	B	C	D	E	F	G	H	I	J	K	L	M
Egyptian about 3000 B.C.													
Phoenician about 1000 B.C.													
Greek about 600 B.C.													

Modern	N	O	P	Q	R	S	T	U	V	W	X	Y	Z
Egyptian about 3000 B.C.													
Phoenician about 1000 B.C.													
Greek about 600 B.C.													

"The World of the Phoenicians" may be modified so as to use it as a review game where student teams need to answer questions before rolling the dice to ascertain their next move.

Follow-Up

Have students use a modern map featuring Mediterranean Europe and North Africa to determine current national boundaries. They should determine which contemporary nations were influenced by Ancient Phoenician settlements.

The World of the Phoenicians Action Cards

Card 1

Travel Directly
to Cyprus

(A)

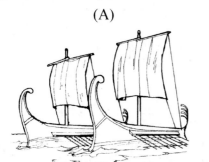

Card 2

Travel Directly
to Sardinia

(B)

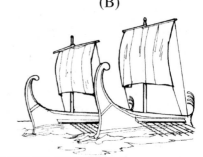

Card 3

Travel Directly
to Crete

(C)

Card 4

Travel Directly
to Asia Minor

(D)

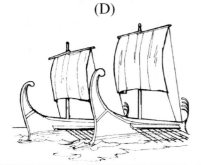

Card 5

Travel Directly
to the East Coast of
the Adriatic Sea

(E)

The World of Phoenicians
Action Cards *(cont.)*

Wild Card

Your ship meets
dense fog.

Lose one turn.

Wild Card

Storm ravages
your fleet.

Lose a turn.

Wild Card

Fair winds remain
behind you.

**Take another turn in
the direction of your
choice.**

Wild Card

Your men have
gathered fresh food
on shore.

**Take another turn in
the direction of your
choice.**

Wild Card

Trade goods are looted
by barbarian pirates.

Lose one turn.

The World of the Phoenicians Map

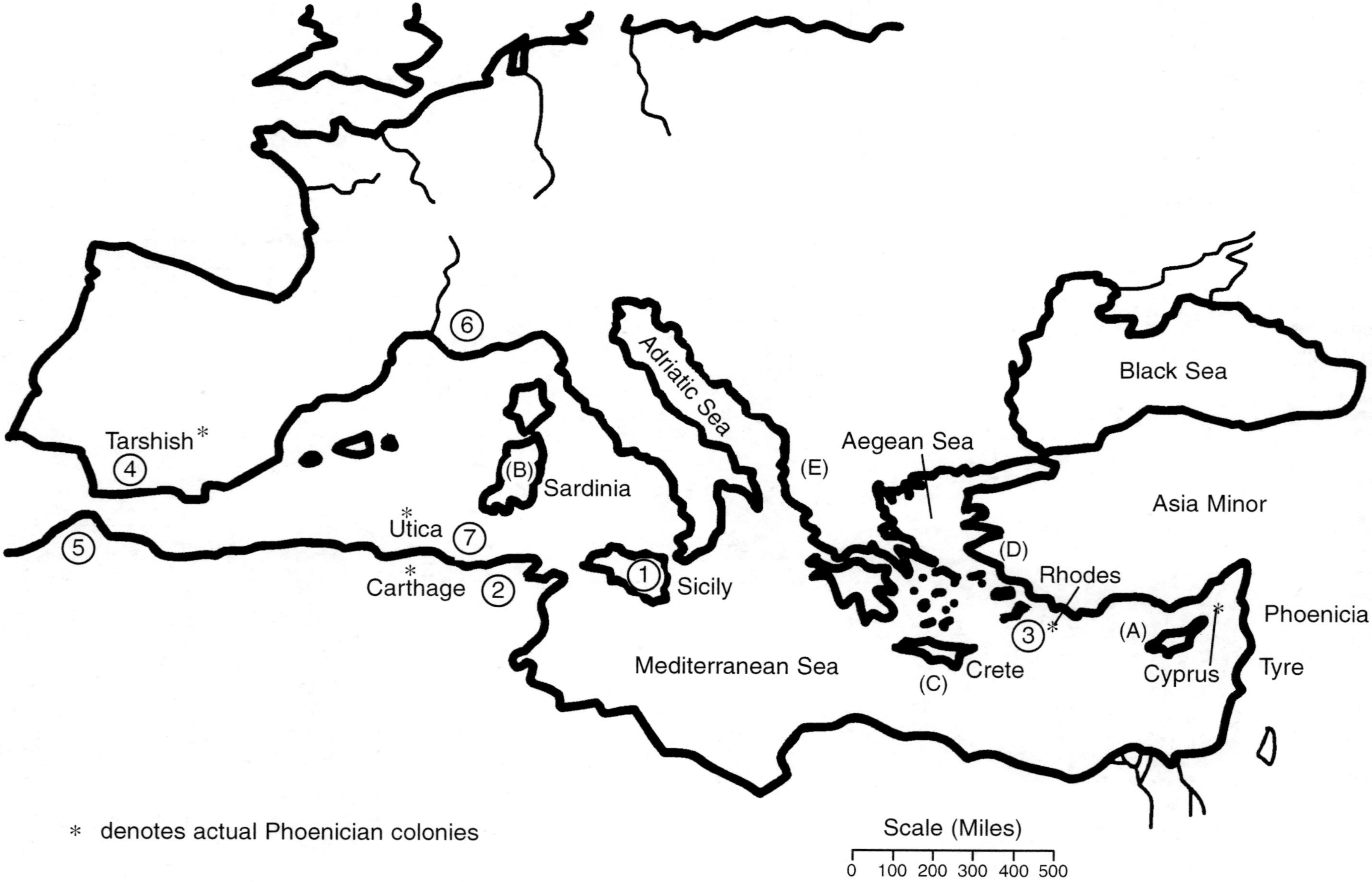

Black Sea

Asia Minor

Phoenicia

Tyre

* Cyprus

(A)

Rhodes

(D)

3 *

Crete

(C)

Aegean Sea

(E)

Adriatic Sea

Sicily

1

Mediterranean Sea

Sardinia

(B)

Utica *

7

Carthage *

2

6

Tarshish *

4

5

Scale (Miles)

0   100 200 300 400 500

* denotes actual Phoenician colonies

Ancient Mariners

Topic

Phoenicians: Latitude and Longitude Skills

Objective

Students will identify the Ancient Phoenicians as the first mariners to circumnavigate the African continent. They will accurately employ latitude and longitude skills in reworking a Phoenician route around Africa.

Materials

- the accompanying map of Africa (page 43)

Preparation

Make copies of the map of Africa for each team of students.

Procedure

1. Divide students into teams of twos or threes and give a map of Africa to each team. (At teacher discretion, students may work at this task individually.)

2. Make known to the class that the Phoenicians were the first known sailors to circumnavigate the continent of Africa some 2,600 years ago. Today you will test their "navigation" skills by having them follow the course of these early mariners through the use of latitude and longitude coordinates.

3. Since the Phoenicians accomplished this feat by sailing out of the Red Sea, have the first coordinate somewhere in that body of water. Have the students label the first coordinate with a number "1." Label each successive coordinate the instructor offers in a similar manner—2, 3, etc. (See the sample map of Africa, page 43).

4. Have somewhere between 10 to 12 coordinates for the students to plot. When finished, the students should connect the points. Samples are given on page 42 with a key on page 44.

5. The instructor should collect the maps and compare them with his/her master copy to see which teams should be honored with the title of "Seaworthy Ancient Mariners."

Ancient Mariners *(cont.)*

Background

The Phoenicians were the most notable sailors of their time. (See "The World of the Phoenicians," page 35.)

Just as modern businesses have to react to increased competition to keep their market share, the Ancient Phoenicians had to compete with Greek traders. This forced the Phoenicians to expand their shipping and trading lanes as far as Britain and West Africa.

Around 600 B.C. an Egyptian pharaoh was curious about what lay beyond the Red Sea. The pharaoh employed a group of Phoenician vessels to sail beyond the Red Sea and follow the coast of the African continent in order to find out whatever they could. The sailors took three years to accomplish the adventure as they went ashore every autumn to plant grain and wait out its harvest in the spring before returning to the sea. They always sailed within sight of land. The Phoenicians were fine seamen, but they were also cautious.

It was a meritorious achievement, considering no other expedition was able to round the southern reaches of Africa again until Vasco da Gama, the Portuguese explorer, rounded the Cape of Good Hope in 1497, more than two thousand years later!

Then again, maybe the Phoenicians planned it that way. One tactic they employed to guard their favorite shipping lanes was to create stories of fantastic sea monsters designed to scare the wits out of prospective competitors.

Coordinates as Indicated on Map of Africa Key (page 44)

1.	20° N,	38° E	8.	2° N,	10° E
2.	13° N,	50° E	9.	7° N,	12° W
3.	0°,	42° E	10.	23° N,	18° W
4.	22° S,	40° E	11.	36° N,	5° W
5.	35° S,	31° E	12.	34° N,	20° E
6.	28° S,	13° E	13.	32° N,	32° E
7.	7° S,	12° E			

Follow-Up

Using seven- or eight- inch lengths of string, students can figure the distances between the various points they plotted. The string will help them negotiate the distances entailed on the curved routes. One inch on the map equals approximately 670 miles.

Ancient Mariners *(cont.)*

Map of Africa

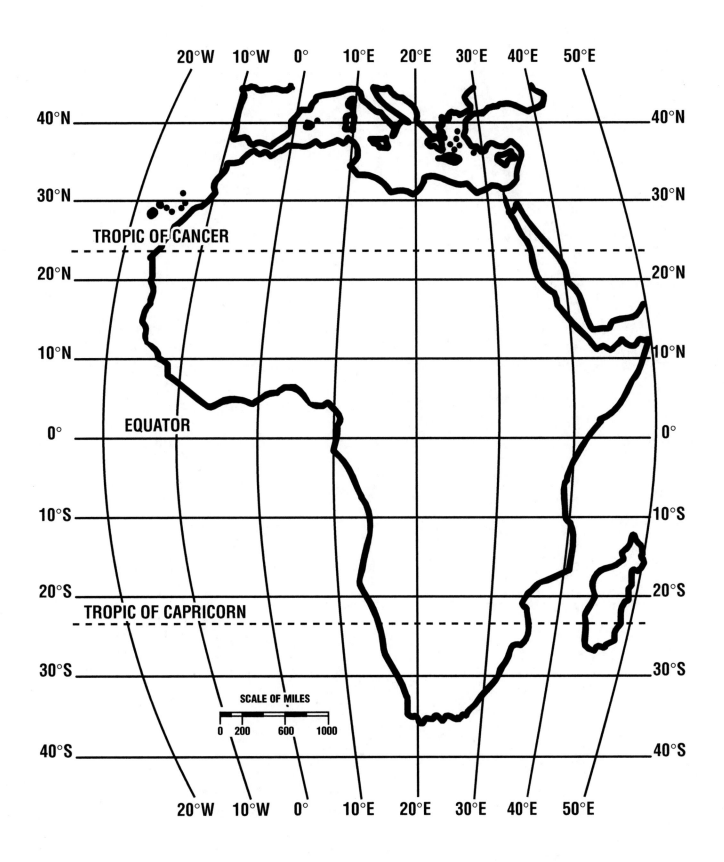

Ancient Mariners *(cont.)*

Map of Africa Key

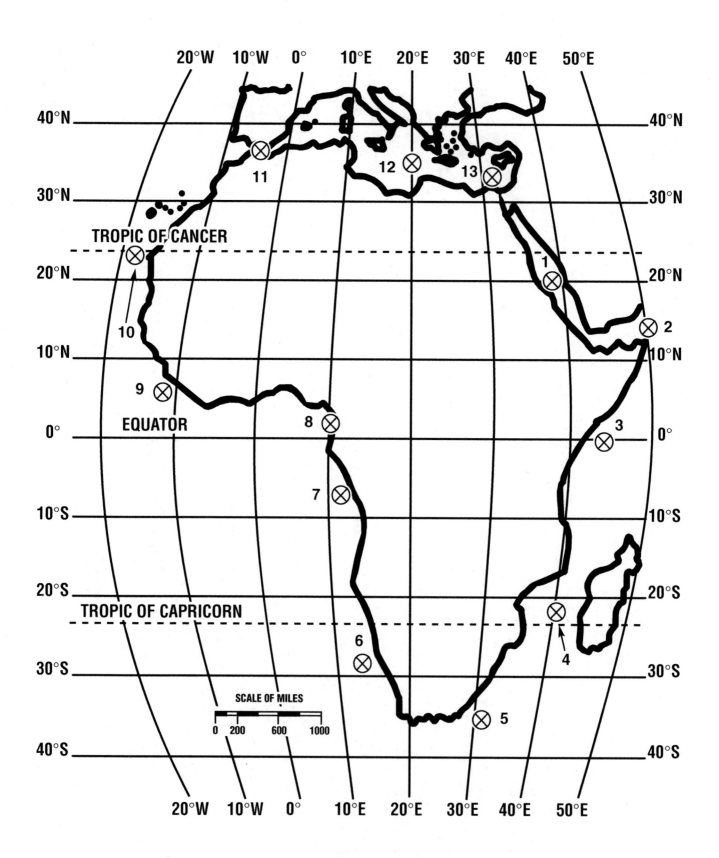

The Bully Dilemma

Topic

The Assyrian Empire

Objective

Students will identify how the Assyrians used brute force and intimidation to expand their empire. They will identify possible strategies to protect themselves from physical intimidation.

Materials

- the accompanying dilemma story, "Jeremy" (page 47)

Preparation

Make enough copies of the dilemma for each student in the class.

Procedure

1. Have the class situated in cooperative groups of four pupils each and pass out the problem-solving dilemma.

2. Orally read the dilemma while the students read it silently.

3. Have students pair off within each team to discuss the questions accompanying "Jeremy."

4. After a few minutes of one-on-one discussion, teams should reconvene and student pairs should share their ideas with each other within the team.

5. When teams have had sufficient time to interact, the teacher should hold a whole-class discussion of the situation within "Jeremy." If the dilemma is being used as a closure lesson on Assyria, a fifth discussion question can be added to those present with the story— "How does this situation compare to the role of the Assyrian Empire in the Ancient Middle East?"

Background

The Assyrian Empire was located along the Tigris River in what today would be northern Iraq. The height of the empire was reached between 800 B.C. and 650 B.C. The Assyrians were farmers who developed into formidable warriors on the arid plains of northern Mesopotamia. Fear of attack from outsiders catapulted their drive to become a fearsome military power.

The advantage of new iron weapons coupled with a ruthless, almost demonic attitude towards their enemies made Assyrian soldiers some of the fiercest fighters of the pre-Christian era. They incorporated terrorism into their military strategy by torturing prisoners and cruelly ravaging the citizenry of cities they conquered. This reputation for brutality often paid off handsomely when opposing forces would simply surrender rather than suffer the consequences of defeat in battle. Later, Assyria extracted tax and tribute from adjacent lands in order to enrich its naturally poor homeland.

The Bully *(cont.)*

Background *(cont.)*

However, by 612 B.C. the Assyrian capital at Ninevah was destroyed by forces from beyond Assyria's frontier. These people took the initiative to destroy Assyria while it was under weakened rulers rather than chance that Assyrian aggression be turned upon them.

In light of Assyria's role as intimidator in the Near East some twenty-eight hundred years ago, the dilemma, "Jeremy," directs the students' frame of mind to a very localized situation of a similar nature. Any student who has experienced physical intimidation from a bully or gang of any sort will relate to the personal terror and anxiety that such an event instills within him or her.

The dilemma may be used as an anticipatory set to introduce Assyria's role in the Ancient Near East. It may also be used as a closure activity where the Assyrian experience is held up for comparison by individual students.

When it comes right down to it, perhaps the most important lesson students can gain from the ancient Assyrians is the one of recognizing intimidation as a cover-up for fear and developing a coordinated action plan to defeat it (with other affected parties). Discussion question number four becomes vital. As difficult as it has been even for modern nations to stop a bully (Europe appeasing Hitler prior to World War II), individuals will have just as much difficulty unless as a group they become resolved to report and resist intimidation.

The Bully Dilemma

Jeremy

Jeremy sauntered into class, a smirk on his face. He had just taken several dollars worth of lunch money from two more students during morning recess. As usual, his plan had worked to perfection. No witnesses were present, and his victims were totally intimidated by his physical stature.

Jeremy hadn't grown up with much at home. His father had left the family of five boys and two girls when Jeremy was very little. In such a large family with limited resources, the younger ones usually were content with the older siblings' leftovers. Clothes, toys, and at times, even food were greedily consumed by the oldest quartet of siblings, leaving the youngest three to fend for themselves from the scraps. Jeremy grew up with this "get it before someone else does" attitude. And grow he did.

By the time Jeremy reached the seventh grade, he was the largest boy in his class. At almost six feet and one hundred fifty pounds, he even dwarfed some of his teachers. Jeremy was well aware of his size advantage and used it to extort money from other students going to, from, and at school. Simply put, if Jeremy marked you, it was either give up your money or get a physical beating. Several times he had severely bruised the face of a student only to deny any involvement whatsoever. Whether luck or skill, Jeremy was able to pick out those kids that he was able to corner for a minute or two alone.

Like a hawk that can notice an isolated mouse from several hundred yards away, Jeremy had a sixth sense about whom to pounce upon and when to do it. His activities, however, didn't go totally unnoticed.

Several other students of questionable character were attracted to the "easy money" Jeremy had latched onto. While not able to contend for the top prize, members of Jeremy's "posse"—some three or four in number—assisted him in picking out easy prey and watching the halls and streets for any trouble while Jeremy was "conducting business." In return, Jeremy shared some of his loot with his band of followers.

In the eyes of his peers, Jeremy was the most feared and powerful student in the school.

Respond to the following questions:

1. If you had to deal with a person like Jeremy, how would you face up to him? What kind of plan could you devise to help protect yourself?

2. What would you like to see happen to Jeremy and his followers?

3. What are the possible consequences that await Jeremy?

4. How can a school or neighborhood protect itself from a bully like Jeremy?

A House Divided?

Topic

The Ancient Hebrews

Objective

Students will identify the reason for the conquest of the Ancient Hebrew nation by Assyria and Babylonia.

Materials

- the accompanying illustration
- six pieces of dark construction paper, 12" x 18" (30 cm x 45 cm)

Preparation

1. Make six copies of the illustration on page 50.

2. Fold each sheet of construction paper in half and insert a copy of the illustration inside the folded construction paper. The illustration may be secured with staples or tape.

Procedure

1. Select six articulate students to come to the front of the class while the remaining students take out a piece of paper and a pencil.

2. Instruct the six students that they are to assume the roles of leaders of a nation (the remainder of the class represents that nation's citizenry). In order to ward off confusion among the people and possible invasion from rival lands, these six must accurately communicate instructions to their citizens. They need to give clear direction for their nation so it will remain united. The task they are about to undertake, while having nothing to do with government, will test their ability to have the citizenry follow their directions.

3. Give each of the six students a copy of the illustration. Tell them that they are to give oral directions to the rest of the class so that all students will recreate the illustration that they possess. Stress that only oral directions will be acceptable. The six may have several minutes to decide exactly how to approach this problem. (**Note:** *During this period of time, the teacher may incorporate some review questions or other sponge activity for the remainder of the class.*)

4. Allow the group of six students a fair amount of time to get the remainder of the students to successfully recreate the illustration. Each class will pose a different situation. Some classes may be very successful within 10 minutes; others may be overly frustrated in a couple of minutes. The instructor needs to gauge his/her class accordingly and allow a seemingly successful session to continue a bit longer, while promptly ending one that is meeting with overt chaos.

A House Divided? *(cont.)*

For Discussion

After the activity has concluded, ask the student leaders what was difficult for them as they were conducting the activity. Ask the class what specific things the leaders did or said that made them successful (or unsuccessful) in communicating the illustration to them. For the entire class, "How might a nation suffer if its leaders cannot successfully direct the people?"

Background

"A House Divided" is designed to be an anticipatory set to the study of the Ancient Hebrews.

Specifically, the instructor will need to transfer the student's focus on the ability (or inability) of the class leaders to communicate to the fall of the Hebrew nation some twenty-seven hundred years ago.

The pinnacle of the Ancient Hebrew nation was under the rule of kings Saul, David, and Solomon (approx. 1020 B.C. to 930 B.C.). Solomon's opulent lifestyle and his numerous non-Jewish wives and their foreign gods led many Hebrews to question the wisdom of a unified government of their 12 tribes.

After Solomon's death, the 10 northernmost tribes formed the kingdom of Israel while the southern tribes around Jerusalem formed the kingdom of Judah.

Internal discontent continued to ferment in each kingdom until the Assyrians overran Israel in 722 B.C. Judah lasted until 586 B.C. when Nebuchadnezzar conquered Jerusalem and took the Jews captive to Babylonia.

American history attests to the consequences of disunity within a nation. However, it need not be so drastic an event as a civil war to weaken a nation. Continual mistrust and miscommunication between a people and their leaders can, over time, serve to ravel the stitches on the cover of national unity.

Depending upon the makeup of the class, the teacher may wish to ask students if they can recognize any issues or events within our nation's recent past and/or present that might serve as examples of things or ideas that have separated Americans rather than having unified them. Within the past generation, Americans have had to deal with an unpopular war that split the nation (Vietnam), the disastrous "Watergate" affair that eroded public confidence in the federal government, and an ongoing public debate regarding abortion.

Finally, as a logistical note, teachers need to be certain that they select six of their more verbal students for "A House Divided?" While it may end up in bickering at the head of the class, such annoyances would be preferable to a silent group too inhibited to present much, if any, direction to the class. In fact, a sextet of strong-willed "Bickersons" might instill proper focus upon the very objective of this lesson.

A House Divided? *(cont.)*

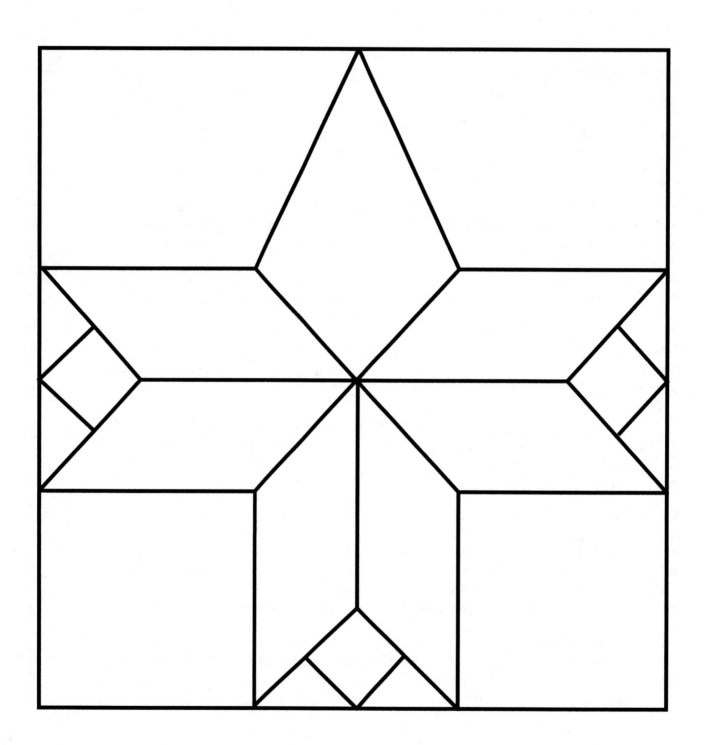

Gracious Victors

Topic

Ancient Persia

Objective

Students will identify the Persian Empire as one tolerant of the differences, religious and cultural, of the people it conquered. They will recognize the benefits reaped from a tolerant society as opposed to an oppressive society.

Materials

- construction paper in three different colors (There should be enough sheets in order to give one sheet per student. There should be equal numbers of sheets for two of the colors while there should only be three or four sheets of the third color. Do not use very dark colors.)

- a large area (outdoors or in the gym) where students can join hands to make a large human circle

- (OPTIONAL) several jump ropes or lengths of rope or wide ribbon (in order to help delineate the inner boundary of the human circle)

Preparation

Procure the various required materials.

Procedure

1. Randomly pass out the construction paper sheets, one per student.

2. Have all students write the following information on one side of the paper:

   - student name

   - two special interests or hobbies they enjoy

   - one specific talent they have

   - what they hope to do as adults

3. Go to an area large enough for the entire class to join hands and form a human circle. (Students should lay their papers in front of them.) The circle will be complete when all students have their arms fully outstretched with hands joined.

4. When the circle is complete, lengths of rope may be used to help form the inner boundary of the circle. The entire inner circle need not be roped—just enough of it to identify the inner perimeter.

Gracious Victors *(cont.)*

Procedure (cont.)

5. At this point, explain to the class that their circle represents a community of people. It could be a nation, a state, a city, or even a small neighborhood. When any group of people within the community is persecuted or harshly picked upon, the community as a whole suffers.

    Explain that the various colors of construction paper represent differences within the community. These differences may be racial, ethnic, religious, or of another nature. At this time, we will see what happens if a small group of people is picked on or discriminated against. Announce that "All students with the (least predominant construction paper color) sheets of paper should release hands and withdraw from the circle."

    The remaining students should see if they can maintain the circle with their reduced numbers. (In all probability, if they were properly spaced to begin with, they will not be able to maintain the circle without leaving several gaps in it.) The circle is broken in the same way that a community remains incomplete and injured when persecution is allowed to persist.

    If students are able to close the circle by reducing its diameter, point out that by doing so they have symbolically reduced the accomplishments the original group was capable of producing. (Use Step #6 to explain this.)

6. Have the students return to class with their papers. Use the blackboard to inventory the students' talents and future career choices (hobbies may be added also if time permits). Place a star next to the talents and aspirations of those students who withdraw from the circle. Ask the class how the community as a whole would suffer if those talents and career goals were shunned by the community.

7. Use the Backround information to interrelate the Persian empire's practice of tolerance with the benefits Western civilization eventually learned and acquired from it.

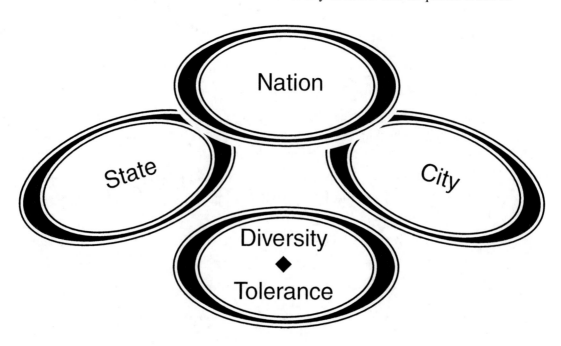

Gracious Victors *(cont.)*

Background

From approximately 550 B.C. to 350 B.C., the Persians dominated the Near East from the Mediterranean and Black Sea to India. In several important regards they were unlike any other conquerors of the region up to that time.

First, leaders such as Cyrus and Darius were extremely tolerant to the peoples that their empire enveloped through conquest. Unlike the Assyrians and other conquerors of the past who sought to terrorize and intimidate their subjugated masses, the Persians allowed cultural and religious differences to flourish as long as political loyalty was maintained.

Secondly, under Darius the first idea of absolute monarchy—a single ruler dictating the administration of the empire from tax collection to the utilization of the military—was introduced.

Darius was able to overcome centuries-old rivalry between valley-dwelling farmers and warlike nomadic herdsmen by incorporating the herdsmen in his army while the farmers were free to produce the required sustenance for the empire at large.

The results of this new use of power were vital for the future of Western civilization. Instead of destroying foreign religions, Cyrus allowed the Hebrews who had been held captive in Babylon to return to Jerusalem and rebuild their temple. Although the implications of faith within this incident can be legitimately pursued, in a purely secular sense, the Persian trait of tolerance helped sustain the Judeo-Christian ethic within the Western world. In addition, the Greeks, eventual conquerors of the Persians, adapted much of what the Persians had learned from others in the areas of government, science, and mathematics. The Persians were able to take the best attributes of their indigenous peoples and mold those into a powerful coalition that continually sought to learn more for the betterment of the empire. Unfortunately for it, a succession of poor monarchs ultimately led the Persians to capitulate to Alexander the Great in the fourth century B.C.

Follow-Up

Teachers may extend the idea of tolerance and learning about other cultures among their own students. The more diverse the community, the greater the opportunities that will exist.

Students may interview another student from a different race, religious background, ethnic heritage, or regional origin within our nation. These interviews may include such topics as foods and social or religious traditions and/or customs.

Students may even wish to attend another family's social or religious event (with permission of their own parents, of course).

Ancient Democracy

Topic

Ancient Greece

Objective

Students will describe which segments of society were included in the original Athenian democracy. They will compare and contrast early Greek democracy to democracy as it is exercised in the United States today.

Materials

- the accompanying role cards (page 57)

Preparation

1. Make enough copies of the role cards so there is the following ratio: Ecclesia cards should number one-half the male membership of the class. Metic and servant cards combined should equal one-half the male membership of the class.

2. Cut out the required number of role cards. (Cards may be laminated for future use.)

Procedure

1. Initiate a discussion with the class regarding an upcoming project. Tell them that you are undecided about what kind of project you want them to do (about any topic you may be currently studying). Explain that you have thought about a report, a diorama, a play, a mural, etc. However, you have decided to let democracy rule on this project.

2. Pass out the needed number of role cards at random to male students only.

3. Explain that only those students who possess an Ecclesia card may enter into discussion about the proposed project.

   As deftly as possible, garner responses only from those boys holding an Ecclesia card. Those boys holding other cards or the girls of the class must be politely, but firmly, told that their opinion in this matter doesn't count.

4. Hold a vote on the project choices, allowing only ecclesia members to vote.

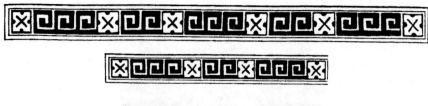

Ancient Democracy *(cont.)*

For Discussion

After eligible voters have made their decision, the instructor may have to deal with some upset students. The following questions may help defuse and clarify the lesson succinctly:

- How was or wasn't this a democratic way of dealing with the project dilemma? (Some students got to vote, but only a minority were able to do so.)

- What part of the classroom membership was totally left out of the decision-making process? (the girls)

- Who among the boys were not able to participate in the "democratic" process? (those with cards marked "Servant" and "Metic")

Inform students that this activity simulates the earliest forms of democracy as it was born in Ancient Greece. Metics, or foreign males, and servants or slaves, as well as women, were denied a part in the governing process. Only those males age 18 and over whose ancestors had been citizens of Athens were given the right to vote. Have students compare those qualifications to modern voter qualifications in our country.

(All citizens—those born in the United States and those legally naturalized—age 18 and older may vote, regardless of race, religion, gender, or political beliefs.)

Ancient Democracy *(cont.)*

Background

The idea of democracy was a radical concept for Ancient Greece of 500 B.C. For over 500 years the Greek city-states had been ruled by oligarchies—small groups of aristocratic men who made all major decisions for the city-state. The Athenian democratic ideal developed methodically, commencing with the great law-giver, Solon, in 594 B.C. and continuing with a civil official named Cleisthenes. By the time Pericles became a significant government official in Athens (461 B.C.), all common male citizens whose ancestors had been Athenian citizens were able to direct the course of government.

Pericles

At the height of its power, Athens had a population of approximately 200,000 people of whom about 50,000 constituted the male citizenry. This citizenry met by tribe on a monthly basis to decide issues handed to them by a more exclusive governing assembly. Large numbers of foreigners and slaves, as well as the women, had no voice whatsoever. In effect, Western man's initial experiment with democracy was extremely limited, since a minority led the majority.

Follow-Up

Check with your local board of elections to see what percent of eligible adults are registered to vote in that area. Also, ask what percent of eligible voters actually cast ballots in the last election. In all likelihood, a self-chosen minority of citizens are making decisions for the majority even to this day.

This could lead to further discussion or an essay for the students, "The Value of a Vote."

The aforementioned Cleisthenes also introduced the concept of ostracism to the ecclesia. The citizenry of Athens could deem a particular person as dangerous to the state and, by a majority vote, have that person exiled for 10 years. If an instructor is open to some controversy and has some advanced students, he or she may pose the question as to what public figure in the United States should be ostracized if it were legal. The debate could be interesting even if the idea is unconstitutional.

Ancient Democracy Role Cards

ECCLESIA

ECCLESIA

ECCLESIA

ECCLESIA

METIC

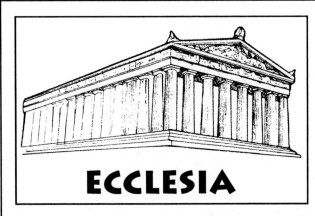

METIC

SERVANT

SERVANT

A Spartan Dilemma

Topic

Ancient Greece (Sparta)

Objective

Students will identify that Spartan civilization was founded upon a militaristic point of view that allowed no tolerance for contrary views or physical limitations.

Materials

- the accompanying dilemma story, "Commander Lear" (page 60)

Preparation

Make a copy of the dilemma for each student.

Procedure

1. Have students grouped in teams of four. Have one student chosen as a team recorder.

2. Pass out the copies of the dilemma. Orally read "Commander Lear" to the class.

3. Have students within each group take turns listing positive qualities of the main character, Commander Lear. The recorder should list these qualities. In a similar manner, have team members take turns listing negative characteristics of Commander Lear.

4. For the remaining questions, have students pair off within each team and discuss them. After pairs have discussed the questions, they should share their responses with the other pair within the team.

5. The whole class should reconvene, and the teacher should review the items of the dilemma by allowing each team to share either their positive/negative qualities lists or their views on one of the other questions.

6. Explain to the class that they will begin learning about a "civilized" Ancient Greek city-state that promoted most of the actions presented in "Commander Lear."

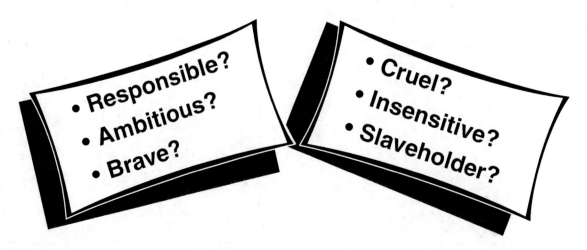

A Spartan Dilemma *(cont.)*

Background

Sparta, Athen's perennial nemesis among the Greek city-states, was founded on the idea of military might producing economic right. Like most city-states on the Greek peninsula, Sparta was unable to support itself solely from the products of the rocky, infertile soil. However, while most Greeks turned to the sea for trade and commerce, Sparta made the conscious decision to aggressively impose its will on neighboring city-states, subjugating their people into forced labor for the benefit of Sparta.

As a result, Spartan society developed into three classes. Spartans were the military faction of society constituting a mere five percent of the people. The vast majority of the people were traders, artisans, and slaves. The former enjoyed some freedoms while the latter had virtually none.

A Spartan male left home at age seven to enter into severe military training lasting until he became 20, whereupon he was considered in active service until the age of 60. While marriage was permitted, no Spartan could live with his wife until the age of 30.

Women were trained to be good wives of soldiers, and the "soft" education of the arts, literature, and philosophy were frowned upon as being unworthy for a warrior. Newborns were examined shortly after birth. Any birth defect or hint of infirmity immediately sentenced the infant to death by exposure, and it was left on a mountainside to die. Imperfect specimens would not be accepted in Spartan society.

"A Spartan Dilemma" is designed to be an anticipatory set prior to the class study of this Greek civilization. If time permits after the study has been completed, the instructor may wish to allow students to make a comparison between the Spartan attitude towards society and Hitler's view of an Aryan "master race" in Nazi Germany. For a more contemporary comparison, these Spartan ideas may be compared to the various supremicist groups that often make the news with their elitist racial diatribes.

Answers to discussion questions (page 60):

1. Answers will vary. Possible answers: responsible, ambitious, successful, brave, respected, caring (towards his son, and perhaps his wife, although the details are thin in that regard).

2. Answers will vary. Possible answers: narrow-minded, cruel, insensitive.

3. This land is very militaristic. The army (at least Commander Lear's portion) moves by foot. It does not value conventional education. Physical strength and stamina are prized almost to a fault. There would appear little room for opposing ideas.

4. Answers will vary.

Commander Lear

The day had dawned with wonderful anticipation for Commander Lear, a leader of one thousand of his land's best soldiers. His young son of seven was to enter the Youth Military Academy, and his wife was expecting another child very soon, perhaps this very day.

Lear beamed with pride as his son was met by Academy officials at the gate. Even though his son would never leave the Academy until the age of 20, the commander knew that to be a tough, disciplined soldier (perhaps an officer someday), academy life was required. It was what he had known. It had developed his skills as a leader of men in a land of bravery. It was what everyone who was truly worthy aspired to accomplish. Real men weren't interested in the art or words of other men; real men ruled other men.

However, his send-off for his son was interrupted by a messenger's panting announcement that his wife's time had come. Upon Commander Lear's return home, the midwife passed him with eyes gazing downward. A wailing in the next room alerted him to sharp emotional, not physical, pain. His wife was sobbing uncontrollably. He entered to find an apparently healthy baby boy comfortably cradled next to his mother.

But all was not as it seemed. His wife removed the blanket to reveal the infant's clubfoot. The right foot was positioned slightly askew, pointing outwardly somewhat perpendicular to his leg. This boy would never be able to march among the legions of soldiers. Commander Lear now fully realized the source of his wife's grief.

Upon notification of the birth of his son, the council elders would visit and inspect the child for physical fitness. This one would never pass inspection, and it would be killed. Inferior physical specimens could not contribute to the society, so they had to be done away with.

Commander Lear quietly walked out of the room. His joyous day soured. Like any good soldier, he followed orders well.

Respond to the following questions:

1. Name any positive characteristics you can detect in Commander Lear.

2. Name any negative characteristics of Commander Lear.

3. From the story, can you infer, or figure out, any information about the land in which Commander Lear lives?

4. What is your overall impression or feeling about the land in which he lives? Could such a place really exist? Why or why not?

United They Stood

Topic

Greco-Persian Wars

Objective

Students will recognize that through a united effort the Greek city-states were able to withstand Persian invasion in the fifth century B.C.

Materials

- the accompanying "checkerboard" map of Ancient Greece (page 66)
- an overhead projector and transparency
- a collection of small plastic discs (small enough to fit in each square on the "checkerboard" map)—eight solid discs and eight transparent discs of various colors
- a bag of candy or other reward
- the accompanying identity cards (pages 64 and 65)

Preparation

1. Make an overhead transparency of the "checkerboard" map.

2. Make a copy of the identity cards and cut them out. You may wish to use heavy stock that can be laminated so that cards may be held for future use. (Once your class is placed in teams of two, half of the teams will be Persians. The remaining teams will take on the identity of individual Greek city-states.)

3. Obtain the discs. (A teacher supply store or catalog that carries math manipulatives would be an excellent source.) Discs can also be made by cutting circular shapes out of colored acetate (transparency film or report covers).

4. Decide upon a reward that will motivate your class and procure it if needed.

Procedure

1. As you are discussing the Persian Wars in Greece, divide the class into pairs of students.

2. Randomly distribute the identity cards and situate the Persian teams on one side of the room and the Greek city-states on the other.

3. Call the class' attention to the overhead screen and the "checkerboard" map of Greece. Denote the solid (black) discs situated on the eastern side of the map. These represent the Persian troops about to advance on Greece.

United They Stood *(cont.)*

Procedure *(cont.)*

4. Call everyone's attention to the multicolored discs on the western side of the map. These are the Greek city-states.

5. Explain to the class that a strategic game of checkers is about to be played out on the overhead screen. The Persians are on one side. The individual Greek city-states have to decide whether they want to play together on one side against the Persians or if they prefer to play alone. If they play alone, they cannot be jumped and removed by another Greek city-state—only by the Persians. In either case the winning side will "conquer" the specific prize chosen by the instructor.

   (**Note:** *To create a Greek king in this checkers game, use a dark marker to place an "X" on the acetate piece. Persian kings may be made by using an odd-shaped piece. That is, if discs are used for the regular pieces, use square or cube-shaped ones for the kings.)*

6. Once the city-states have determined what each will do, proceed with the game of checkers. If the city-states unite, play a normal game, designating team captains to announce their moves which the teacher will make.

7. However, if some city-states prefer to go it alone, allow separate turns for each to make their moves against the Persian forces.

Background

Around 500 B.C. the Persian empire was spreading its influence into the northern regions of modern Greece. When the local citizenry revolted with assistance from several Greek city-states, the Persian leader, Darius, set out to punish the intervening Greek cities. This led to a two decades-long war highlighted by several momentous military campaigns.

United They Stood *(cont.)*

Background (cont.)

In the first campaign, Athens single-handedly held off Persian forces on the plains of Marathon in 490 B.C. Later, in 480 B.C., 31 Greek city-states joined in a combined effort to turn back a determined Persian force under Xerxes. In the sea battle of Salamis, a large Persian fleet was defeated by a smaller Greek flotilla. Ultimately, Persia withdrew its military from the Greek mainland and relented in its attempt to expand further westward.

"United They Stood" cannot guarantee a Greek victory in checkers, of course. However, the activity should reinforce the concept that cooperation among many in the face of a severe crisis is preferable to working in isolation.

Follow-Up

An interesting footnote to the Greek victory over Persia is that among the unified city-states, Athens gradually became the preeminent power. By demanding tribute from other cities to help prepare to ward off any further Persian incursions against the Greeks (even though the threat was no longer real), Athens grew extremely wealthy at the expense of other city-states. Worse than her financial usurpation of these city-states was that Athens, home of democracy, had eliminated their political rights in an attempt to placate its own citizenry that had become accustomed to the river of wealth flowing into Athens. Ironically, by the end of the fifth century B.C. a Spartan-Persian alliance brought Athens to its knees.

If the instructor wants to emphasize this footnote in history, allow only the team of students representing Athens to control the prize distribution (assuming the Greek city-states emerge victorious in the checkers match).

United They Stood Identity Cards

PERSIANS

PERSIANS

PERSIANS

PERSIANS

PERSIANS

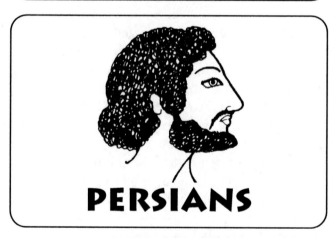

PERSIANS

PERSIANS

PERSIANS

United They Stood Identity Cards *(cont.)*

 **SPARTA**

 **ATHENS**

 **CORINTH**

 **DELPHI**

 **OLYMPIA**

 **THEBES**

 **PELLA**

 **AMPHIPOLIS**

 #2102 Ancient History Simulations

United They Stood Map

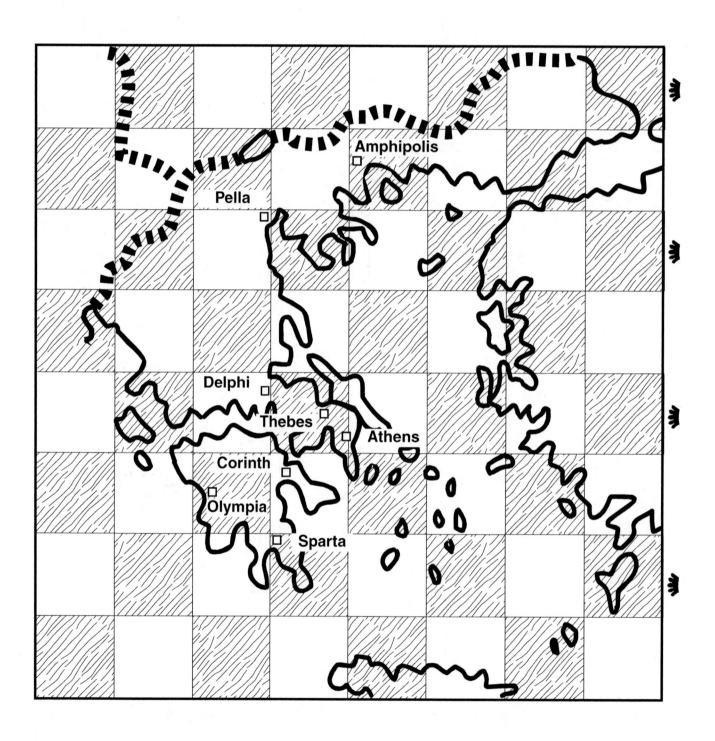

Amphipolis

Pella

Delphi

Thebes

Athens

Corinth

Olympia

Sparta

An Enduring Encyclopedia

Topic

Ancient Greek Advancements in Learning

Objective

Students will incorporate library research skills in identifying that Greek advances in various sciences were the benchmark for knowledge in the Western world for over 1500 years.

Materials

- the accompanying list of Ancient Greek scientific scholars (page 69)

- a set of teacher-directed instructions for the corresponding research project (See Procedure step #2.)

- an individual volume or an entire set of an old encyclopedia (optional)

Preparation

1. Develop a specific set of instructions for the research project alluded to in step #2, Procedure.

2. Make copies of the instructions and the list of Ancient Greek scientific scholars for each student.

Procedure

1. Have students grouped in cooperative teams of four.

2. Use the list of Greek scholars as a basis for a research-oriented project. The instructor is free to set the parameters of the project to meet the instructional needs of the his/her students. Some possible options include the following:

    A. Have teams divide the list. Each student will research two names on the list and prepare a written report which will be employed in an overall group report on these ancient intellectuals.

    B. Have each student in a team draw a name of one person on the list. All students within the class with a specific Ancient Greek scholar work together to research and annotate information on that person. When research is complete, each student reports his/her findings to their original teams.

    C. More advanced students may be able to incorporate information from all these famous names into one written or oral report.

    D. Student teams may also present visual and/or oral presentations with a written report. Bulletin boards, murals, video "interviews" with the ancient ones, dramatized debates concerning relative concepts the early scientists supported, etc., are possible formats for students to explore.

3. After individual or group presentations have been completed, ask the class the following question: "If you had your choice between a 1950's encyclopedia or one published last year to use as research for a project, which would you choose?" (If you have an old encyclopedia, you may hold it up as you are presenting the question.)

An Enduring Encyclopedia *(cont.)*

Procedure *(cont.)*

Allow the students the opportunity to answer the question with specific rationales for their answers.

(Many students will use the newest version of an encyclopedia for the most current information. Some may argue that the topic in question may make either edition just as valuable.)

4. Use Background to inform the class of the Ancient Greek origins of encyclopedias. After having highlighted this data, ask "What does the fact that Greek scientific knowledge was the basis for European knowledge for over 1500 years tell you about the Ancient Greek scholars? What does it tell you about Europe from the birth of Christ to about 1500 A.D. (the Renaissance)?" (Students should note that the Ancient Greeks were gifted in their study of natural occurrences while scientific investigation stagnated in the "Dark Ages" of Europe. Learning was coveted by the Greeks while the Romans pursued conquest and post-Roman Europe just sought survival.)

Background

The word *encyclopedia* comes from the Greek *enkyklios paideia*, "in a circle of instruction." Even though Aristotle is credited as being the originator of the first encyclopedia, the oldest original version still intact is the *Historia Naturalis* (Natural History) which dates to 79 A.D. It was compiled by a Roman, Pliny the Elder, and centered on the natural sciences of mathematics, geography, anthropology, physiology, botany, and zoology. It consists of 37 books including almost twenty-five hundred chapters.

While compiled by Romans, the basis of scientific knowledge in these encyclopedias of the first and second centuries A.D. was of Greek origin in the five centuries prior to the birth of Christ. It remained the unadulterated source of scientific intellect for over 1500 years. Not until the work of Copernicus and Galileo in the sixteenth century did significant new discoveries either complement or displace the work of the Ancient Greeks.

The profusion of scientific discovery in the Greek world during the five centuries before the birth of Christ is considered the second greatest era of scientific detection in the history of the Western world. It was not surpassed until the relatively modern era of the past four centuries.

The listed Greek scholars are noted below with approximated life spans and fields of study:

Greek Scholar	Life Span	Field of Study
Democritus	(460–370 B.C.)	atomic theory
Pythagoras	(582–500 B.C.)	number theory
Hippocrates	(460–377 B.C.)	medicine, anatomy
Aristarchus	(310–230? B.C.)	astronomy
Hipparchus	(185–120? B.C.)	astronomy, trigonometry
Euclid	(323–285 B.C.)	geometry
Archimedes	(287–212 B.C.)	geometry, physics
Eratosthenes	(275–200? B.C.)	geography, mathematics

ANCIENT GREEK SCHOLARS

- **DEMOCRITUS**

- **PYTHAGORAS**

- **HIPPOCRATES**

- **ARISTARCHUS**

- **HIPPARCHUS**

- **EUCLID**

- **ARCHIMEDES**

- **ERATOSTHENES**

Harassing Hannibal

Topic

The Punic Wars Between Rome and Carthage

Objective

The students will accurately use map scale while locating places associated with the Punic Wars and/or reviewing general knowledge about Ancient Rome.

Materials

- the accompanying map, "Rome vs. Carthage" (page 73)
- an overhead projector
- an overhead transparency and marker
- a set of review questions about Ancient Rome (optional)
- rulers for student use

Preparation

1. Make copies of the map for each student.
2. Make an overhead transparency of the map.
3. Procure the overhead markers and make sure students have easy access to rulers.

Procedure

1. Have students situated in cooperative teams of three or four.
2. Randomly assign teams to "Rome" or to "Carthage." The Roman "legions" (teams) should outnumber the Carthaginians by a two-to-one ratio.
3. Pass out the student maps of "Rome vs. Carthage."
4. Explain to the class that you are going to ask them to use the map scale to determine the distance between Rome or Carthage and 11 political/physical features on the map that were important in Hannibal's assault against Rome. The features are numbered but not labeled.

Students may use any text or reference material to assist in determining the correct number for the selected feature.

Roman teams will figure the distance in miles to the specified site from Rome. Carthaginian teams will do the same from Carthage. Round to the nearest $\frac{1}{4}$" when measuring to calculate distance. The first side to offer the correct distance from their city to the selected site controls that site. There will be 11 sites in all, so controlling six features constitutes a victory. (**Note:** *Have students measure from the designated point on the map for their city to the closest point of the circle surrounding the number of the site in question. Although answers given in Background are calculated to the nearest quarter inch, the instructor will need to allow for minor variations.*)

Harassing Hannibal *(cont.)*

Procedure *(cont.)*

5. Copies of the chart below may be distributed to teams for their use in the contest. Use the following descriptors for announcing the various features:

Give the distance from your city to . . .

A. the Kingdom of Macedonia   G. the Land of Gaul

B. the Island of Sicily   H. the Island of Corsica

C. the Island of Sardinia   I. the Adriatic Sea

D. the Pyrenees Mountains   J. the Alps Mountains

E. the Ionian Sea   K. the Land of Spain

F. the Po River

Descriptor	Distance from Rome inches	miles	Distance from Carthage inches	miles
A.				
B.				
C.				
D.				
E.				
F.				
G.				
H.				
I.				
J.				
K.				

Harassing Hannibal *(cont.)*

Background

The Punic Wars were a series of three conflicts between Rome and its archrival in the western Mediterranean Sea, the city-state of Carthage (present-day northern Tunisia). The first ended with Rome seizing Sicily in 241 B.C. The last totally destroyed Carthage in 146 B.C. At this point, however, we note the Second Punic War (218 B.C.–201 B.C.) where the rugged determination and inspirational leadership of one man, Hannibal, almost brought Rome to her knees.

Hannibal took a force of some 50,000 men from Spain over the Pyrenees and Alps and invaded Italy in a bold attempt to eliminate Rome. He lost almost a third of his men to the elements and barbaric mountain tribes. Incredibly, he led his army to rout after rout of Roman forces within Italy where he fought for 15 years. Eventually Roman strategy called for mere sniping and delaying tactics until legions outside of Italy put enough pressure on Carthage to have it recall Hannibal, which occurred in 203 B.C.

"Harassing Hannibal" may be used straight up to highlight physical sites involved in his epic war with Rome after students have studied it. It could also be used to review Rome in general. Alternating review questions could be given to both sides as precursors to the specified sites for which distances need to be determined. Please note that only 11 of 20 numbered sites on the map are used in the activity.

Harassing Hannibal Answer Key

Descriptor		Distance from Rome inches	miles	Distance from Carthage inches	miles
A. # 1	Kingdom of Macedonia	1 1/2''	450	2 1/4''	650
B. # 2	Island of Sicily	3/4''	250	3/4''	250
C. # 3	Island of Sardinia	1/2''	150	3/4''	250
D. # 6	Pyrenees Mountains	1 3/4''	550	2''	600
E. #10	Ionian Sea	1 1/4''	400	1 1/4''	400
F. #11	Po River	1/2''	175	1 3/4''	550
G. # 9	Land of Gaul	1''	325	1 3/4''	550
H. # 4	Island of Corsica	1/2''	150	1''	325
I. #15	Adriatic Sea	3/4''	225	1 3/4''	550
J. #14	Alps Mountains	1 1/4''	400	2 1/4''	700
K. # 8	Land of Spain	2''	600	1 3/4''	550

Harassing Hannibal Map

Rome vs. Carthage

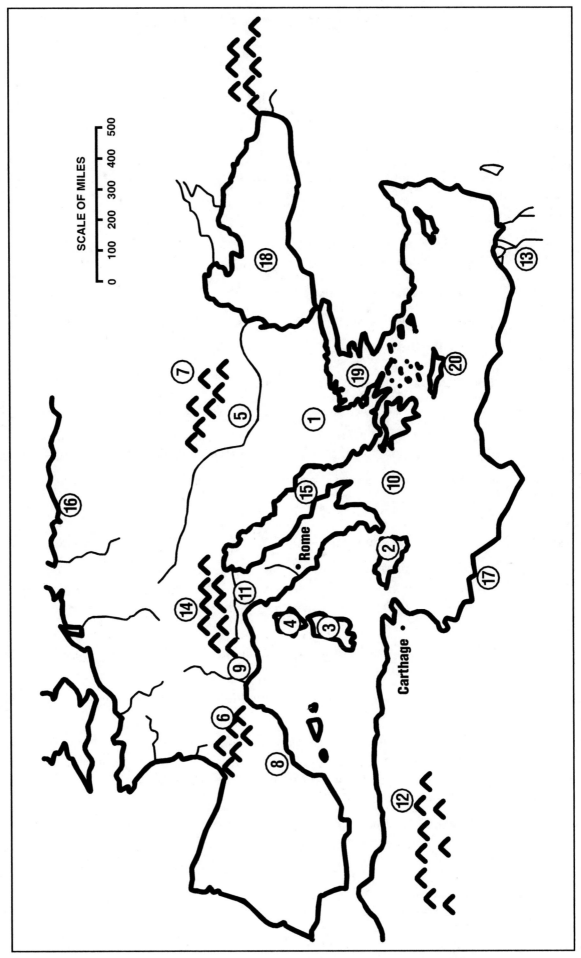

SCALE OF MILES

0 100 200 300 400 500

Rome

Carthage

Class Conscious Review

Topic

Social Classes of Ancient Rome

Objective

Students will identify the major social classes of Rome and their roles in supporting the empire.

Materials

- the accompanying social class cards (page 76)
- a set of teacher-created review questions
- the accompanying set of Roman coinage (page 76)
- an edible treat (optional)

Preparation

1. Make a copy of the class cards and cut them out. (For future use, laminate the cards.)
2. Duplicate sufficient Roman coins. (Correct answers in the review activity will merit one coin each. Note that some coins possess a value of five and others of ten.)
3. Prepare review questions over the previous lessons on Ancient Rome.

Procedure

1. Have students divided into cooperative teams of three or four pupils each.
2. Randomly distribute the social class cards.
   (**Note:** *Have no more than one group as "Patricians." There should be at least two groups of "Provincials." "Plebians" and "Slaves" should have at least one student team each.*)
3. Employ review questions on a rotating basis. With each correct response, reward the team with a Roman coin.

   (These coins may represent a specified treat, such as a certain amount of candy, if the instructor so desires.)
4. When the review questions have been completed, each team should tally its rewards in coins. At this point, the following tribute (or tax) must be forwarded. "Provincials" need to give one-half of their money to the "Patricians." "Slaves" turn over all their coins to the highest class of Rome.
5. Should an optional treat be redeemable, the redemption should occur after all taxes and tributes have been collected by the "Patricians."

Class Conscious Review *(cont.)*

For Discussion

Many students will cry "foul" at the outrageous taxes and tribute imposed at the end of the review activity. Focus the class attention on what has (presumably) already been learned about Roman society:

❑ Which was the dominant power-wielding class within Rome? (patricians)

❑ Who provided the lion's share of wealth to Rome? (tribute collected from various foreign provinces whose people had no right to Roman citizenship)

❑ Who did Rome depend upon for the majority of its soldiers and artisans? (plebeians)

❑ Who provided most of Rome's physical labor force? (slaves)

Background

Simulation #19 (Class Conscious Review) makes no pretense of being fair. It attempts to replicate the social strata of Ancient Rome. While the taxation percentages are arbitrary, they are not without purpose. The patricians were the elite of Roman society, the aristocratic wealthy with a long Roman lineage.

The plebeians were the common folk of Rome who, though not materially endowed, still enjoyed the honor of Roman citizenship. They paid taxes, but their greatest value to the patricians was their ability to fill the ranks of the military. Slaves bore the brunt of labor within Rome and had virtually no legal standing. Finally, the people of the various Roman provinces throughout the Mediterranean region paid hefty tribute to Rome and had no rights to citizenship within the empire (at least none until near the end of the empire's reign).

Class Conscious Review Class Cards

PATRICIAN

PLEBIAN

PROVINCIAL

SLAVE

Hail to the Chief Dilemma

Topic

Augustus Caesar's Reign over Rome

Objective

Students will realize that beginning with Augustus Caesar, the emperor of Rome inherited his title and could rule in an absolute manner. They will identify specific portions of our Constitution that would prohibit relinquishing the people's power to vote and have their say in government.

Materials

- the accompanying dilemma story, "Eugene Jones, Imperial President" (page 79)

Preparation

Make a copy of the dilemma for each student.

Procedure

1. Place students in cooperative teams of four each.

2. Before introducing a lesson on Augustus Caesar, distribute "Eugene Jones, the Imperial President" to the class. Orally read the dilemma to the class or have the students read it silently.

3. Have teams break into pairs to address the discussion questions that follow the dilemma.

4. When pairs have finished the questions, have them share their responses with the other pair within their team.

   (**Note:** *Teachers may wish to allow students a bit of research time in order to investigate specific aspects of the Constitution of the United States.*)

5. When group work has been completed, have a whole class review of the discussion questions. This should lead directly into the lesson(s) concerning Augustus (see Background, page 78).

Hail to the Chief Dilemma *(cont.)*

Background

Augustus Caesar, also known as Octavian, was the adopted son of Julius Caesar. When the latter was murdered by Roman senators, Augustus shared power with Mark Antony. For over a decade Augustus ruled Rome's western regions while Antony reigned in its eastern corridor near Egypt. A power struggle eventually did ensue in which Antony was killed and Augustus took supreme power.

Several years into his reign, Augustus forfeited all his powers to the Senate and the people. Having suffered from nearly a century of sporadic civil war and impressed by his abilities to rule the diverse people and geography that was the Roman empire, citizens and government officials alike were eager to keep Augustus at their helm. While his initial resignation did restore a representative democracy to Rome, the Senate and citizenry used their restored rights to vote Augustus extreme powers to control the state. He was first tribune for life (a position that oversaw the assembly of common citizens) and controlled the consuls of the Senate. He also was supreme commander of the military.

Central to this lesson is the fact that the majority of Roman citizens felt it easier to give one man total reign over their empire rather than depend upon their republican institutions to do so. (Perhaps 100 years of civil strife would do that.)

However, through "Eugene Jones, Imperial President" students should become aware of the safeguards inherent in our Constitution and the potential dangers of failing to exercise our freedoms. If one forfeits one's rights, then it should come as no surprise when one no longer holds any power.

Possible answers to the questions on page 79:

1. Jones has reduced unemployment and crime. He has helped business profit and strengthened the military.

2. The citizens of the nation have given up responsibility.

3. President Jones seems to have been given a good deal of power. Note the national police corps and the way protests, though minor, have been handled.

4. Article II (electoral college) as well as Amendment 12; Amendments 15, 19, 26 dealing with voting rights; Amendment 22 dealing with term limits for the President and Vice-President.

Eugene Jones, Imperial President

It is January 20, 2057, and Mr. Eugene Jones has just been sworn in as President of the United States for an unprecedented fifth term. In fact, as in each of his last two terms, there was no election. Mr. Jones was voted in by acclamation of the House of Representatives. How could anyone become President of the United States without an election?

During Jones' first term, he was able to dramatically reduce unemployment to a point where just about everybody who wanted a job was able to get a good job. He was able to work so well with business leaders and Congress that while unemployment was vanishing, business profits were booming. The stock market increased its value by almost 40 percent during Mr. Jones' first four years.

In Jones' second term, he strengthened the military and reduced taxes. He was able to do this because so much new business was created in his first term that the government was finally able to get out of debt for the first time in nearly 70 years.

Furthermore, just about every segment of American society loved Eugene Jones. How could they not love a man who helped improve nearly everyone's standard of living! There seemed to be no threat to America within her borders or from any foreign land. All nations were duly impressed with her might with Mr. Jones leading her.

Then eight years ago, someone floated a seemingly unthinkable idea in Congress. Forget about having another time-consuming, expensive, and divisive presidential election. Why not alter the Constitution to remove the two-term limit for the president? Even more radical was the idea to eliminate voting on the presidency altogether—too costly, not necessary. Everyone wanted Eugene Jones! So Congress voted to have the House of Representatives vote every four years to renew his "contract" to run America. He had done so well that there wasn't any real opposition. Oh, there was some, but those persons were dealt with so effectively that no one ever took the matter to the Supreme Court. In his third term, Mr. Jones started a national police corps which used the total power of his office to stop crime wherever it existed. New prisons were built, and thousands of enemies to the prosperity of the nation were put away. Again some protested the manner in which courts were run, but most people were content with Mr. Jones' style. He got things done!

Respond to the following questions:

1. What good things has President Jones accomplished?

2. Who has given up their responsibility in this situation?

3. What possible problems could arise if such a situation actually did occur?

4. What parts of the United States Constitution are violated in this story?

Mound Builders Network

Topic

Hopewell Culture of North America (circa 300 B.C.–600 A.D.)

Objective

Students will identify trading patterns among the Hopewell cultures.

Materials

- the accompanying map of the Hopewell trading network (page 85)
- the accompanying resource cards (pages 83 and 84)
- an overhead projector
- two overhead transparencies

Preparation

1. Make an overhead copy of the trading network map.
2. Make sufficient copies of the resource cards and cut them out. Seven copies of each resource (one copy for each student team) should be enough. Laminating them will allow for future use. (**Note:** *Greenstone will need twice as many copies as the other resource cards.*)
3. Make a transparency of the accompanying resource/products chart (page 82).

Procedure

1. After some introductory lessons on the mound building cultures, place the students in cooperative teams of four.
2. Present the trading network map on the overhead and randomly assign selected tribes from the map to a particular student group. These teams will role-play their assigned tribes in a trading simulation.
3. Each team (tribe) will be given seven resource cards each of the one or two resources identified with them on the map.
4. Using the transparency of the accompanying list of tools and products (see Background, page 81), each team should select three tools or products that their tribe might benefit from having but do not have the resources to make. These resources will then be the specific targets of trade that the tribe will go after. Each team is to present its list of three needed items to the teacher before trading begins.
5. On the teacher's command, teams may begin to trade according to the following basic guidelines:
   - Teams may dispense given resources among all members.
   - Teams may allow members to spread out and trade individually.
   - Teams may also choose to remain together to trade.
6. Periodically, teams may regroup to ascertain how they are progressing to meet their trading goals. When a tribe has acquired the necessary resources to create the three tools or products it thought useful to have, it should consider its trading excursion a success and withdraw to its original seating area.

Mound Builders Network *(cont.)*

Background

Often referred to as a "mound building" culture, the title "Hopewell" actually characterized a trade network among native people of the eastern two-thirds of America as much as it described their penchant for erecting ceremonial and burial mounds. Just as one would understand the existence of numerous inherent differences between groups of people linked together by the broad label "European," so too the Hopewell encompassed a variety of people. Among the Hopewell, diverse in language and customs, trade and the use of mounds was a common link.

❑ **Copper** from present-day Minnesota (People of the Far North) was used for ornamental jewelry (earrings, bracelets) as well as utilitarian items such as fish hooks.

❑ **Flint** (or chert) from the Ohio Valley (Serpent Mound People) was the major source of spear points and knives.

❑ **Pipestone**, a reddish clay-like rock from which elegant effigy pipes were carved, was also located in the Ohio Valley.

❑ **Obsidian**, a glassy volcanic rock from the Rockies (Land That Touches the Heavens), was the premier cutting material. Its razor-sharp edge made exceptional filleting knives and scrapers.

❑ **Grizzly claws**, also from the Rockies, were used in necklaces.

❑ **Shells** and **fossilized sharks' teeth** from the Gulf of Mexico (The Salt Water Sea) were prized as ornamental trinkets.

❑ **Greenstone**, a type of igneous rock, was used to shape adze heads. It was found in southern regions (Father of Waters, Land of the Sunrise).

❑ **Mica**, the seemingly translucent, layered mineral which was valued in making amulets, was also found in the southern regions.

❑ **Silver** was found in present-day southern Ontario (The Freshwater Sea People).

"Mound Builders Network" is a very active undertaking. It is not for those who wince at the thought of much student movement throughout a room. The activity also needs an adequate foundation in previous lessons on the mound building cultures as to their locations, tools, products, resources, and needs.

Resources/Tools and Products Chart

Resources	Tools and Products
copper	fish hooks, earrings, rings
obsidian	knives, scrapers
grizzly claws	ornamental necklaces
mica	amulets (charm necklaces)
greenstone	adze heads, hatchet heads
pipestone	pipes
flint (chert)	spear points, knives
seashells	ornamental trinkets
sharks' teeth	ornamental trinkets
silver	jewelry

Mound Builders Network
Resources Cards

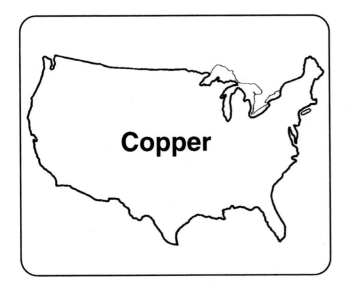

Copper

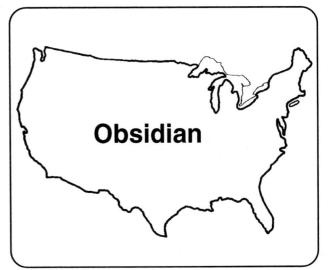

Obsidian

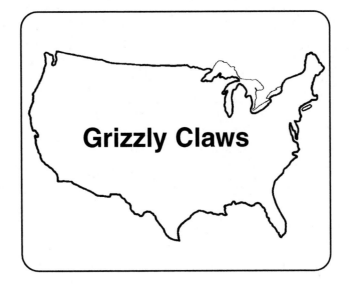

Grizzly Claws

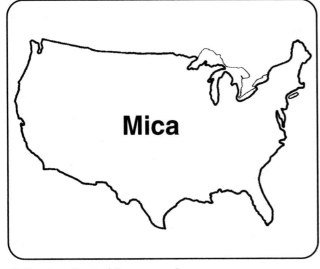

Mica

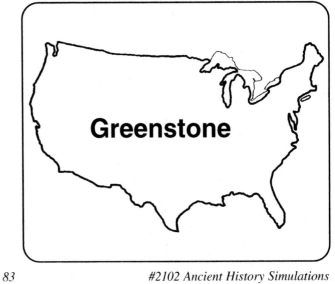

Greenstone

Mound Builders Network
Resources Cards *(cont.)*

Pipestone

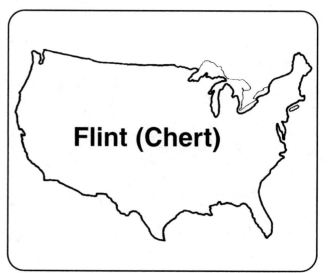

Flint (Chert)

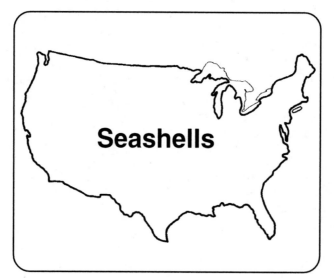

Seashells

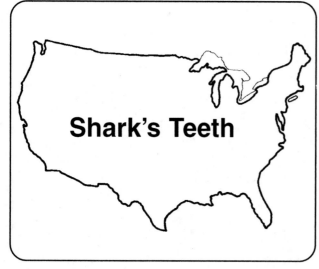

Shark's Teeth

Silver

The Hopewell's Trading Network

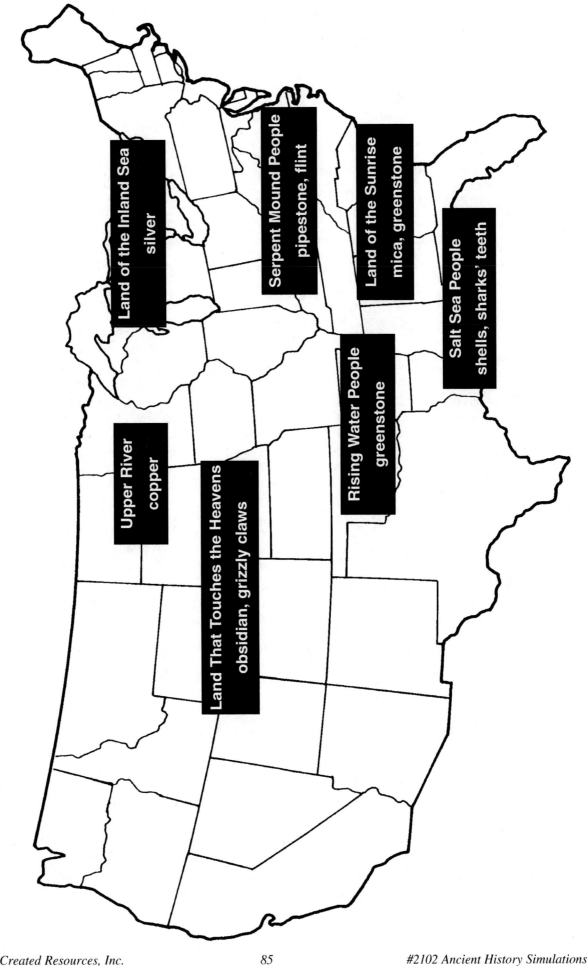

Land of the Inland Sea
silver

Serpent Mound People
pipestone, flint

Land of the Sunrise
mica, greenstone

Salt Sea People
shells, sharks' teeth

Upper River
copper

Land That Touches the Heavens
obsidian, grizzly claws

Rising Water People
greenstone

Urban Planning

Topic

Ancient Mayan Civilization

Objective

Students will describe and explain the significance of the building plan of a Mayan city.

Materials

- the accompanying set of Mayan societal class cards (page 88)
- the accompanying class seating diagram (page 89)
- an overhead transparency (optional)
- an overhead projector (optional)

Preparation

1. Make enough copies of the cards to allow for two Priests, Nobles, Artisans, and Merchants each. The remainder of the class should receive cards marked Peasants. You may wish to use heavy stock that can be laminated so that cards may be held for future use.

2. Using an overhead transparency or the chalkboard, recreate the seating diagram so students can easily position themselves according to its layout.

Procedure

1. Use the sample diagram to reposition the desks in your room before the students arrive for the start of the day. (**Note:** *The sample is set to a standard rectangular room formation; feel free to improvise the seating to meet your individual room configuration. It is only necessary to maintain the concentric effect of Priests/Nobles in the center followed by an outer ring of Artisans/Merchants with Peasants on the exterior fringes).*

2. As students enter the classroom, randomly dispense the role cards one by one.

3. Instruct students to view the seating diagram and sit in any position that corresponds to their specific role cards.

   (**Note:** *You should be sure to collect the role cards once all students have been properly seated. This is especially important if you teach in a departmentalized format where several classes will enter your room throughout the course of a day.*)

4. Before the instructor proceeds with the day's lesson about the Mayan civilization, he or she should inform the students that the peculiar seating arrangement represents the layout of a typical Mayan city. The teacher may ask students to offer conjecture as to the significance of this residential pattern. (See Background, page 87.) Depending upon the content of previous lessons, students may readily offer an accurate explanation, or they may just hypothesize if "Urban Planning" is being used as an anticipatory set for information that is to be initially presented on that day.

Urban Planning *(cont.)*

Background

The Mayan civilization of southern Mexico and northern Central America (Guatemala, Belize) reached its height between the third and tenth centuries, A.D. Its cities were focal points of religious celebrations involving pyramid-style temples and the worship of numerous gods. Government was conducted and priests and rulers lived in these communities as well.

To that end, the hub of a Mayan city was its temple with priests residing close by. Since nobility ruled, ruling families also lived close to the city's center. With declining status, people lived farther away from the core of the city. Wealthy artisans and merchants resided farther out than the ruling classes, yet they were much closer than the multitude of peasants. They were farthest removed as they took care of the fields on the perimeter of a city.

Once again, "Urban Planning" takes some flexibility on the part of the teacher. For a day, it offers a bit of variety to the class(es) as it attempts to illuminate one aspect of life in a once dominant civilization.

Urban Planning Societal Role Cards

Priests

Nobles

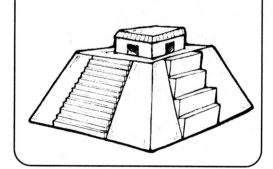

Artisans

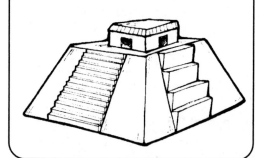

Merchants

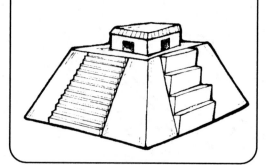

Peasants

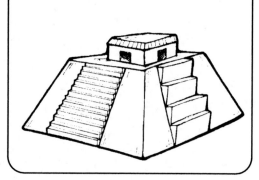

Peasants

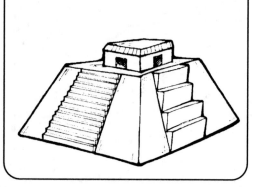

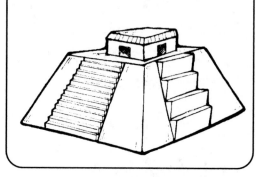

Urban Planning Seating Diagram

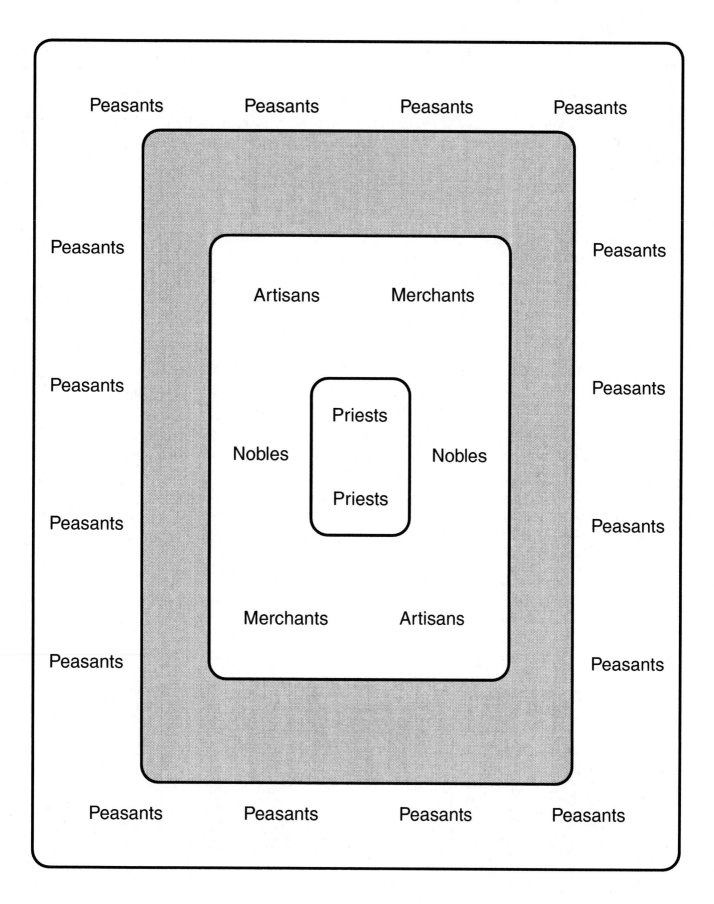

Burning Books

Topic

Ancient Mayans—The Mystery

Objective

Students will identify a major reason Ancient Mayan civilization has been so difficult to understand.

Materials

(No materials are necessary. See Background, page 91.)

Preparation

A visit to the local public library may be in order to procure a more extensive list of banned books and authors. (See Background, page 91.)

Procedure

1. Place the following book titles on the chalkboard: *Mickey Mouse, Charlie and the Chocolate Factory,* The Bible, *James and the Giant Peach, Alice in Wonderland, My Brother Sam Is Dead,* and *A Wrinkle in Time.*

2. With students aligned in cooperative teams, allow them several minutes within teams to brainstorm possible connections or similarities among the listed book titles.

3. After a class discussion in which team spokespersons share possible connections among the books, inform the class that each of these books has been banned in a public or school library at one time somewhere in the United States. If time permits and students are generally familiar with several of the titles, they may be asked to offer possible rationales for the banning of these seemingly benign works.

4. Use the discussion engendered by this activity to lead into a lesson on the way the Mayan civilization (and its demise) of some eleven hundred years ago remains such a mystery. (See Background.)

Burning Books *(cont.)*

Background

As the Spanish conquest of Latin America escalated in the latter part of the sixteenth century, Franciscan missionaries and priests were determined to convert Mayan natives to Christianity by whatever means necessary. Some church officials felt the need to stoop to the use of torture, executions, and total eradication of objects associated with the Ancient Mayan religion. In this fervor, most of a series of books depicting Mayan hieroglyphic symbols, known as codices, were burned because they were viewed as heresy. Of the several dozen codices, only a few remain today, having mysteriously ended up in various European museums over the centuries. It is the accounts of the Spanish missionaries who burned the codices, as well as the few books that survived, that are credited with much of what has been deciphered of the Ancient Mayan language. However, so much of the Mayan language has been unintelligible through the years that one genuinely wonders what a difference the majority of the codices could have made in unraveling the riddle of the Maya.

"Burning Books" is intended as an anticipatory set specific to the issue of the enigma surrounding Mayan civilization. However, with the contemporary concern over the limits of censorship within public schools and libraries, teachers may tie the lesson into a broader theme that looks at censorship through the ages.

The titles included in this lesson were chosen from a list of banned books. Most Americans would never view these specific titles as ones to be eliminated from public circulation. However, if the teacher would like a more extensive list from which to select books, please visit your local public library or write to the following address:

> The American Library Association
> Office for Intellectual Freedom
> 50 E. Huron St.
> Chicago, Illinois 60611

One variation on this lesson could be to list the following authors who have been banned (internationally and/or nationally) at one time or another and have the students deduce their connection to each other:

- Walt Disney

- Albert Einstein

- Shakespeare

- Socrates

- Hans Christian Andersen

- Galileo

Wheeler Dealer

Topic

Ancient Mayans and Aztecs

Objective

Students will identify barter as the major means of economic transaction in the Ancient Mayan and/or Aztec civilizations.

Materials

- a set of teacher-created review questions
- 16 brown paper lunch bags
- six small bags of corn chips
- six bars of chocolate
- four bananas
- two sandwich bags full of fish crackers
- an unopened box of table salt

Preparation

1. Create the review questions over recent lessons on Mayan and/or Aztec civilizations.

2. Number each lunch bag with a dark marker consecutively from one to 16.

3. Procure the necessary materials and place the items into the lunch bags as follows:
   - one chocolate bar in each of six bags
   - two bags of corn chips in each of two bags
   - one bag of corn chips in each of two bags
   - one bag of fish crackers in each of two lunch bags
   - the box of salt in one bag
   - two bananas in one lunch bag
   - one banana in each of two lunch bags

Procedure

1. Have students paired in teams of four for the review activity.

2. As student teams correctly answer questions during the review, allot that team a point next to their names on the chalkboard.

3. After the review questions have been exhausted, the team with the most correct answers would be able to pick out up to five numbered lunch bags. (They are not to be opened until the teacher distributes all the bags and gives instructions as to their use.) The team with the second highest total of correct responses would be able to select four bags, the third place team three bags, etc. Numbers of teams in a class may vary, so each teacher may feel free to alter the number of bags each team receives; however, every team needs at least one.

4. Before the groups open their bags, the teacher should inform them that they contain items often traded at Aztec (Mayan) markets. As soon as they are directed by the instructor, they may look at what they have and what other teams have. Then they may enter into trade, or bartering, to see if they can obtain items from other teams.

Wheeler Dealer *(cont.)*

Procedure (cont.)

5. After a few minutes of trading has transpired, gain the class' attention. Tell the students that one item among all the items in today's "market" was more valuable than the others. Since salt was needed not only to flavor cooking but even more importantly to help maintain physical stamina and health, every team without salt needs to give some food items (one quarter of a chocolate bar, for instance) to the team holding the box of salt. (**Note:** *The box of salt is to remain closed and sealed. If traded, it should be in this original condition and then returned to the teacher at the end of the lesson. Other items are meant to be consumed by the students.*)

Background

The marketplace of an Aztec or Mayan city of central or southern Mexico and northern Central America was the pulse of these Meso-American cultures. In major Aztec cities, up to 60,000 people would crowd the markets several times weekly. Vegetables (maize was the predominant food of the masses), fruits, copper axes, feathers, and even specially prepared puppies which were considered delectable edibles, were offered for trade.

Busy Mayan markets also featured cocoa beans, shells, salt, fish, animal skins, and cotton cloth. In both cultures cocoa beans served as a version of small change to equal out trade transactions. However, in the Mayan civilization some dishonest traders mastered counterfeit cocoa beans. Husks were removed from shells and filled with sand. The false beans were then mixed in with the real cocoa beans.

"Wheeler Dealer" incorporates some of the more obvious materials present in these ancient marketplaces to stimulate a sensory experience for students. Classes that are easily over-stimulated may not be the most suitable candidates for this activity. However, most students will come away from the activity with a significant understanding of the economic system of the Aztec and Mayan civilizations.

Follow-Up

As a spinoff on the idea of counterfeit cocoa beans, remove the chocolate from several mini-sized chocolate bars, taking care to replace the wrapper to make it look like a whole piece of candy. In an appropriately placed review segment of a lesson, offer the fraudulent edibles as rewards for correct answers.

When students receive their bogus awards, discuss the idea of the counterfeit cocoa beans. Students may research what punishments may have been in store for such a perpetrator when he or she was caught.

Incan Bonus

Topic

Ancient Incas of South America

Objective

Students will identify what the purpose of Incan government was and give one example as to how it was implemented.

Materials

- an assorted group of review questions originating from whatever source(s) lessons on the Incans were presented—textbooks, filmstrip, class notes, etc. (Have six questions per every team of four students.)
- Incan bonus review cards (page 96)

Preparation

1. Take the review questions (from whatever source the instructor finds most viable) and type or write them out on a sheet of paper or directly on copies of the review cards on page 96. Leave adequate space following each question.

2. Cut out each question so that it appears on a single strip of paper if you wish to tape or glue them to the review cards on page 96.

   (**Note:** *For a classroom of 24 students, the teacher would use 36 questions—six student teams of four times six questions per team.*)

Procedure

1. Employ the review questions in a general recap of the Incan civilization a day or two before a test on the unit. Have students placed in cooperative teams of four.

2. Each team is to receive six of the questions which appear on six individual strips of paper. (For purposes of the activity, it is best that each team gets consecutively numbered questions such as 1–6, 7–12, etc.)

3. Allow time for each team to answer their six questions as a team. While there are several ways to accomplish this, dividing the team into pairs of two to answer each question is quite effective. After a set of two or three questions has been answered, the pairs compare notes to ensure that the correct answer has been obtained. When all six questions have been accurately answered, the team review is complete.

4. Collect all questions and initiate an oral quiz review where teams receive rotating questions and correct answers are awarded points. In this oral review, teams are subject to any question that was passed out except the six that were its responsibility. In this manner students are exposed to the entire scope of the review.

5. After the game is completed, return only two originally answered questions to each team. The remaining four (24 total in this example) will be kept for "community use" on the test date.

6. During the test, randomly pass out one question per student (from the 24 that were retained by the teacher) that the student may use as a "bonus" answer on the test.

Incan Bonus *(cont.)*

Background

The Incan civilization that lived in Andean South America some 600 years ago had a very communal aspect to its government. The notion that everyone should be prepared to help each other permeated a large part of their culture. Specifically, taxes owed the government were paid in a variety of ways—labor, military service, and food. Male leaders of families were liable to be drafted into military service until almost the age of 50, while several months a year were devoted to societal labor projects. However, while householders were gone, neighbors chipped in by helping that person's family with their field work so their crops would not perish.

It is, however, with food that "Incan Bonus" is most closely aligned. Approximately two-thirds of an individual Incan's harvest was commandeered for government storehouses. This was not out of greed or capricious design. On the contrary, the reserve of food was hoarded in order to protect the people in time of need when food would be judiciously dispersed.

Individual instructors may not agree with the idea of doling out bonus points on a test. One may substitute the test bonus with a general review assignment covering a set number of the questions alluded to in the activity. A bonus question may be offered up for such a homework assignment.

Incan Bonus Review Cards

Incan Bonus Review

_____

_____

_____

_____

Incan Bonus Review

_____

_____

_____

_____

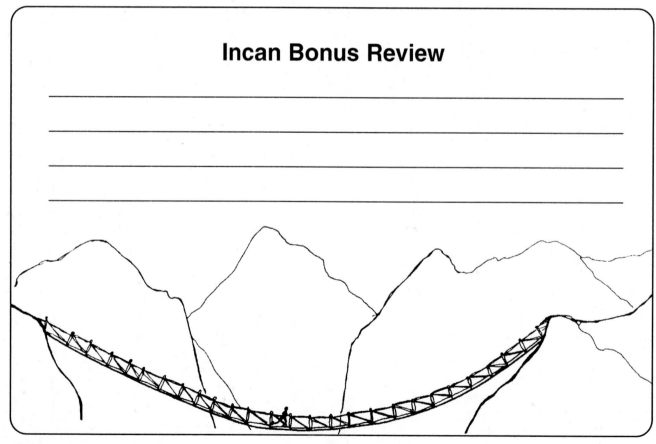